T0338135

SOME CATHOLIC WRITERS

SOME CATHOLIC WRITERS

Ralph McInerny

ST. AUGUSTINE'S PRESS
South Bend, Indiana
2007

Manufactured in the United States of America.

1 2 3 4 5 6   12 11 10 09 08 07

Library of Congress Cataloging in Publication Data
McInerny, Ralph M.
Some Catholic writers / Ralph McInerny.
p. cm.
ISBN 1-58731-777-X (hardcover: alk. paper)
1. Catholic authors – Biography.
2. Authors, English – 20th century – Biography.
3. Authors, American – 20th century – Biography.
4. Authors – 20th century – Biography.
5. English literature – Catholic authors – History and criticism.
6. American literature – Catholic authors – History and criticism.
7. Catholic literature – History and criticism.
I. Title.
PR120.C3M35 2006
808'.8921282 – dc22   2006010311

∞ The paper used in this publication meets the minimum requirements of
the American National Standard for Information Sciences – Permanence of
Paper for Printed Materials, ANSI Z39.48-1984.

ST. AUGUSTINE'S PRESS
www.staugustine.net

CONTENTS

PREFACE

THIS little book is about Catholic authors. More or less. I add that because at least one of the writers discussed was not a Catholic. The inclusion of Willa Cather is justified in the discussion of her. But your wonder may be more basic. Why this odd conjunction of Catholic and Author?

Authors can of course be gathered in many ways, eventually into the bosom of Abraham, let us hope, but in the interim they can be brought under various more or less random categories – Indiana authors, Irish writers, Black poets, unpublished prison penmen. A book devoted to a few Catholic writers may seem at least as quirky a taxonomic tour de force as any of these. But all such adjectival lists suggest a contrast between the authors considered and, well, real authors. Those in the mainstream. Those who are writers *simpliciter loquendo, sans phrase*, as such. There may be such special groups as I have mentioned, the sotto voce suggestion is, but serious talk about writers begins when such restrictive designations become irrelevant.

When I was a boy I received as a Christmas gift a hefty volume titled *An Anthology of World Poetry*. It was edited by Mark Van Doren, and I still have it, more than half a century later. Clearly, to be considered as world class must be the dream of any poet. And yet when you open the book you find subdivisions – Greek and Latin poetry, French and German, English and American. Broad as the net Van Doren flung might have been, it will strike you that whole areas of the globe go unmentioned. In any case, and more relevantly, it becomes clear that the only way to become a world poet is by being a regional poet, just as one lives in the world only by dint of occupying some definite space-time coordinates. It can be argued – I am sure it has been – that all writing is regional writing, specific to time and place, here rather than there, now rather than then. Parochial, even. It is just that the qualities of some writers transcend their age and region.

We live in a time when unquestioned certainty about who qualifies as more than a regional writer seems gone. Quarrels over the "Canon" seem as endless as those over what is called the "peace process." The accusation is made that some petty set of standards lies behind the designation of some writer as part of literature. "Literature" is only a label for one set of arbitrary criteria as opposed to others. We are told that one must be a dead white male in order to make the club. An odd charge, no doubt, since none of the three characteristics amounts to an accomplishment. Still, if you are Black, female, and alive, I suppose you could feel excluded.

I mention this skirmish in the ideological wars because it involves the charge that the movement away from particularity is not in the direction of transcendent qualities. *Of course you were raised by a nomadic band and subsisted on blubber and melted snow as you inched across the tundra, but your sonnets speak to everyone!* Maybe a little skepticism about who gets to inhabit the literary pantheon is not a bad thing. In any case, it has always been a matter of argument and taste as to who is great. One man's immortal may well have feet of clay for another. But I suppose that, in the past at least, disagreement took place within a more fundamental agreement. It was not that the criteria for what counts were up for grabs, but the application of them. "Is Walt Whitman a good poet?" "Can anyone read a novel of Dreiser's for enjoyment?" Such questions need betray no doubt as to what poetry or the novel is. One is quibbling over putative instances.

C. S. Lewis, in a delightful little book called *Experiment in Criticism*, addressed the question, What is literature? He was a professor of literature who had noticed the almost medicinal use of the term. Something could count as literature only if it involved pain in the reading. Meanwhile, everyone, including professors of literature, are poring over books that they would insist do not qualify as the real stuff. It is a good read, entertainment, this or that, but literature? Certainly not. Lewis wondered if we know what we are talking when we say such things. What is literature?

Whatever you will read again. That is the answer Lewis proposed. It is a preliminary answer, but it proves to be a fruitful suggestion in his hands. What is it that brings us back again to a story? Chances are it will not be to find out how it comes out. Surely we remember that. But the plot – the beginning, middle, and end – is a vehicle that carries other things, diction, character, setting, theme, arcane lore, on and on. To enjoy again such things is what leads us to pick up again a book we have already read.

The great merit of Lewis's suggestion is that it supplies a plurality of elements which turn out to be the criteria invoked when we say that a book is more than mere amusement or entertainment. It is one we want to keep, or at least have available in the library. And there can be many reasons, not just one, for that. And degrees are possible in each of them, as well as cumulatively. The plot itself might provide the reason. Say it suggests how easily crucial encounters might not have taken place, the way in which intention and accident blend in the lives of the characters. But many elements of literature can combine to provide a deep reason for re-reading. A favorite author will have a special voice, a distinctive vision. He gives us an intimation of what it all means, of the profound significance of the human actions recounted in the story. A Thomas Hardy tells us stories of fatalistic gloom, but there are moods in which we go back to him, as we go back to the Matthew Arnold of *Dover Beach*. Not because we would care to adopt the outlook on life either of these authors conveys, but because we recognize them as possible ways to interpret events, to see life.

Literature as you and I and C. S. Lewis understand it is important just because it addresses the large questions of human life. This can be done soberly or comically. It may be Joseph Conrad we pick up in the certain expectation that we are going to be taken once more into a world where moral choice and character are decisive. It may be Evelyn Waugh who leads us laughing past the graveyard – or in one hilarious book, through it. Both Conrad and Waugh were Catholics, and like Muriel Spark, had a lively sense of the Four Last Things, the stakes of life. The authors considered in this little book have a Catholic alertness to the ways in which we damn ourselves or accept the terms of salvation. Of course one does not have be a Catholic writer to have such depth, but it helps. It is all but definitive of the authors discussed here.

The point I have made, then, is that Catholic authors, at least those discussed here, can be counted on to deliver what we go to literature for. That is why they are not on the margin of something, on the banks of the mainstream. They occupy its very center. Religious faith is an enormous advantage for a writer. Of course it can also lead to extremely bad writing. Lilies that fester smell worse than weeds. But it is no accident that the atmosphere in which our literature grew and thrived was one where religious faith and its underscoring of the eternal importance of timely deeds was the very air that was breathed.

What makes a bad Catholic writer is a large subject and will not detain us here. You will wonder why the writers discussed below were chosen. The thirty-five authors treated do no exhaust the genre of Catholic writer. Even if I confined myself to the twentieth century, why didn't I write of Conrad? Where are A. J. Cronin and Rumer Goden? Where are Borges and Richard Sullivan? Agnes Repellier and James Gibbon Huneker and Arthur Conan Doyle? How could I have not included Maurice Francis Egan and Ronald Knox? Where are Maisie Ward and Frank Sheed, to say nothing of Ronald Firbank and Sigrid Undset? Did I overlook Malcolm Muggeridge? And, if Flannery O'Connor, why not Caroline Gordon, Alan Tate and Robert Lowell? Oscar Wilde and Theodore Dreiser? Katherine Ann Porter and Dorothy Parker?

All these and many others will occur to you, and I am glad they do. I might have written of writers who were fascinated by

Catholicism, feeling it at once an attraction and a temptation. Henry James and Ralph Waldo Emerson, perhaps Longfellow. And what of those deathbed conversions are re-conversions – Wallace Stevens, Jean Paul Sartre, Borges and Tocqueville. I began but did not finish an account of M. Raymond, the Trappist writer eclipsed by Merton but whose books were once read aloud in seminary refectories across the land. But I could not locate enough of his books to refresh my memory. Nor could I include Francis Finn, S.J. whose novels gladdened the hearts of parochial school children during the 1930s: *Tom Playfair, Percy Winn.* I could find them nowhere. There are several editions of *The Office Boy,* but it did not seem typical to me.

The fact is that the authors discussed are personal favorites of mine. In discussing them, I have given reasons I trust are not merely personal for that liking. I imagine a reader who already knows many of these authors and can find enjoyment in reading about them. A modest goal, except that the enjoyment I imagine is not merely a diversion.

MAURICE BARING

His Catholic characters play minor roles, yet his operatic
friend Ethel Smyth found his novels full of theology.

IN the National Portrait Gallery in London there is a painting by
Sir Henry James Gunn featuring three Catholic authors, two
seated at a table, the third standing slightly behind them. The
massive caped figure on the left, engaged in sketching, is Gilbert
Keith Chesterton. Looking on from the right, hands clasped, sits
Hilaire Belloc. Even now, years after their deaths, they would be
immediately recognized by many. But who is the tall bald figure,
cigarette in hand, watching Chesterton sketch? His name is
Maurice Baring.

It is a name one encounters in reading about others, as for
example in the exchange of letters between Evelyn Waugh and
Lady Diane Cooper, in lives of Belloc and Chesterton, Max
Beerbohm, Ronald Knox, in accounts of the nineties, always it
seems a background figure, in the picture, but standing, not
seated, famous by association rather than achievement. This is
not fair.

Nor would it be entirely true to say that he has been forgotten.
Thirty years ago, Edmund Wilson wrote a testy essay called,
"How Not to Be Bored by Maurice Baring." In 1968, Paul Horgan
published a little pamphlet called *Maurice Baring Reconsidered* and
followed it up in 1970 with a collection called *Maurice Baring
Restored*. Horgan, a lifelong bachelor like Baring, predicted a
Baring revival. It never happened. And yet, in Joseph Epstein's
1993 collection of essays, *Pertinent Players*, is to be found "Maurice
Baring and the Good High Brow," a piece up to Epstein's high
standard.

Maurice Baring was born in 1874 into an upper class family – his father was the first Lord Revelstoke –, attended Eton, which he loved, and went on to Cambridge, where he was marginally associated with the Apostles. (In an essay on Gilbert and Sullivan, he mentions attending a performance with Lytton Strachey.) His extraordinary capacity for languages led him into diplomacy. In preparation, he put in time at Oxford and then crammed in London for the examinations, which he passed only on the third attempt, largely because he was enjoying life in town.

His diplomatic career was brief, and was passed in Paris, Copenhagen, and then Rome. In 1904, he decided to devote himself full time to writing, something the family's affluence permitted. He went off to Russia as a war correspondent to cover the Russo-Japanese war, and fell in love with a country shrouded in mystery. He became fluent in the language and in a literature not yet appreciated in the West, and wrote of it, and translated it. The influence of Chekhov can be seen in Baring's totally natural style. In the first World War, he served in the air corps and was described as the best aide a general ever had. One could fill a book with tributes to Baring, as a friend, as a writer, as a diplomat, soldier, journalist, critic. He seems never to have made an enemy.

Baring was converted to Roman Catholicism in 1909, "the only action in my life which I am quite certain I never regretted." The description that fits him best is man of letters. He wrote some fifty books, verse, plays, essays, linguistic pastiches, anthologies, stories, novels. The three best novels, huge, are *C*, *Cat's Cradle*, and *The Coat without Seam*. "Reading Baring's novels," Epstein writes, "one sees the influence of the religious approach to life on literature, and discovers both its strengths and weaknesses." The novels tell of unhappy loves and convey the sense of the *lacrimae rerum*, that life is, in the end, "*almost* intolerable."

"The point of life is – I think – its imperfection. The point of human beings to me is that they are full of faults and weaknesses and wickedness – it is because of all that they are human . . ." Thus a character in *C*. And there is always the "unexpected goodness, and unexpected badness." His Catholic characters play minor roles, yet his operatic friend Ethel Smyth found his novels full of theology. During his last year, Lady Diana Cooper wrote of a visit to him. "We both felt so gay, sipping sherry, and nibbling chocolate, and arguing about the Pope." She might be describing her exchanges with her much younger friend, Evelyn Waugh.

Baring's autobiography, *The Puppet Show of Memory*, as well as the odd title, can be found in used bookstores. He is a joy to read, but it must be said that he wrote of what was at hand, without apology, and with a graceful ease that keeps the pages turning. He flourished in a time when the entertainment to be found in books occupied a far larger portion of people's lives than it does today. Would his essays now be wasted on the desert air of a televised talk show? Baring himself saw how "what is called Education" was depriving the world of readers. Horgan spoke of a "small and active underground, so to speak, devoted to his work." And so it has remained.

From youth, he was given to triolets and later composed telegrams of them.

> My lines do not scan
> I most heartily grieve
> Quite smooth once they ran
> My lines do not scan
> For the telegraph man
> Refused to abrieve
> My lines do not scan.

He also exchanged verse letters with his dear friend Belloc. Monsignor Ronald Knox was another friend and admirer. Epstein remarks on how unconcerned Baring seemed to be about the reception of his work, yet he expressed astonished delight when he was told of Franáois Mauriac's praise of his novels. He sang, he played the piano, he wrote, he read. He was a type already grown strange in his lifetime, and all but unimaginable now – a Henry

James character, a guest lolling in the library, without visible employment, always busy, yet somehow aimless.

Baring developed Parkinson's Disease in the 1930s and his last years were years of suffering. They were spent at his place in Rottingdean he called Halfway House. Laura Lovat's account of his final days ends thus:

> At a quarter to eleven Fr. McGuire lit the candles on each side of the Crucifix at the foot of his bed, and gave him Final Absolution, and we recited the Litany for the Dying.
>
> At eleven o'clock Maurice died.
>
> Fr. McGuire stood up and said the Magnificat.

It was December 14, 1945. He had ended his last book, *Have You Anything to Declare?*, with these lines:

> *Et à l'heure de ma mort soyez le refuge de mon âme étonnée et recevez-la dans le sein de votre miséricorde.*
>
> At the hour of my death be the refuge to my astonished soul and receive it in the bosom of your mercy.
>
> Amen.

HILAIRE BELLOC

"Her face was extremely broad and flat, and I had never seen eyes set so far apart. Her whole gait, manner, and accent proved her to be extremely good, and on the straight road to heaven."

Of St. Thomas More, Hilaire Belloc wrote, "But this much is certain, that of all those, and they were many, who bore witness in the five generations it took to root out their age-long religion from among the English, his would seem to have been the most complete passion; for he had nothing to uphold him except resolve."

You will find this in a little book called *Characters of the Reformation*. Belloc saw the Reformation as an unmitigated disaster, for Christendom as well as Christianity, and he never let the English forget how they had been led into schism. His portrait of More gives the martyr an unwonted relevance to our own times. More received no comfort from the hierarchy; only the Bishop of Rochester stood fast against the king. There is a lot of Belloc in Belloc's portrait of Thomas More.

Belloc was another layman whose loyalty to the Church was absolute. His youthful book, *Path to Rome*, recounts a hike he made to the Eternal City from the town in France where he had done his military service. It acquaints us with a man of strong opinions, hearty appetites, and lively faith. And it acquaints us with the distinctive voice of Belloc. "And entering I saw one of the women whom God loves. She was of middle age, very honest and simple in the face, kindly and good. She was messing about with cooking and stuff, and she came up to me stooping a little, her eyes wide and innocent, and a great spoon in her hand. Her face was extremely broad and flat, and I had never seen eyes set so far apart. Her whole gait, manner, and accent proved her to be extremely good, and on the straight road to heaven."

Belloc always sounds that sure, about things great and about things small. We sometimes hear of the "triumphalism" of the pre-conciliar Church. Often this means merely the grateful confidence that one holds the true faith. On that basis, Belloc could be the patron of triumphalists. Alas, it is a dwindling band. Or, more accurately, a very different Church is touted where it is sometimes difficult to distinguish belief from unbelief. Christians feel less impulse to go teach all nations when it is intimated that in their own way the pagans have the Good News already. When Belloc was present one always knew there was a Catholic in the room, although an usher once kept pestering him to take a pew until Belloc swore at him. "I'm sorry, sir. I didn't realize you were a Catholic." Not many people made that mistake. When he ran for Parliament, Belloc brandished the rosary he said everyday so that if his constituents objected he would be spared the indignity of representing them.

It would be difficult to find a literary genre in which Hilaire Belloc did not excel, yet he is probably more read nowadays as a poet than as historian or novelist or essayist. And not just the serious poet he was, but perhaps even more as the author of comic verse for children. He was also artist enough to make his way across the continental United States doing portraits when he was on his way to San Francisco to woo the woman who would become his wife.

To think of Belloc is to think of G. K. Chesterton and Maurice Baring, but of the three it may seem to be only Chesterton who is still widely read. Belloc has fared better than Baring, but he may seem to have fallen into obscurity.

It is certain that he is not read as much as he should be, but it would be wrong to think of him as neglected. No Collected Works is planned to match what Ignatius Press is doing for Chesterton, but he has attracted biographers. Robert Speaight's remains the standard, but the volatile A. N. Wilson has written a balanced life that, among other things, puts Belloc's alleged anti-Semitism to rest.

Belloc is said to have published a hundred books. Most of them are out of print and indeed difficult to find. But a surprising number are available in new editions. His prescient essay, *The Servile State*, is available from the Liberty Fund in Indianapolis, with a preface by Robert Nisbet. *The Cruise of the Nona*, easily one of his most remarkable books, has never been out of print (there is a Penguin edition). His *Complete Verse* was reprinted in 1988. Because of the number and variety of his works, it is not easy to get a fix on Belloc.

Half French, married to an American, Belloc was nonetheless quintessentially English. His style is pellucid, a model of clarity, logical progression, and elegance. It is a supple instrument, adaptable to prose and poetry, fact and fiction, journalism and history; one always reads Belloc with a sense of the inevitability of the phrasing. But this is on reflection. It is *what* he has to say that comes through first and powerfully.

Despite his enormous output, Belloc's career can seem a series of frustrated hopes. He had hoped to become a fellow of an Oxford college and spend his life as a teacher. He spent two terms in Parliament and came away soured on what modern democracy was becoming. Belloc, either as professor or as politician, would have been a lesser Belloc. Even his writing came to seem more of a means than an end, the way to earn his bread, book following book. The comic poems, particularly those for children, were serious only in the way comic verse is. Still it was his ambition to be a poet that was unequivocally realized, however little his accomplishment is acknowledged. Let this triolet suffice to suggest its quality.

The young, the lovely and the wise
Their face is set toward their going.
They pass me with indifferent eyes,
The young, the lovely and the wise,
And fill me with a long surmise
Upon my losing and my owing.
The young, the lovely and the wise
Their face is set toward their going.

But it is the rollicking Belloc that has kept his name alive and will bring him back to a new generation of readers. This – and I end with it – is the end of his song on Pelagius.

Now the Faith is old and the Devil's bold,
Exceedingly bold indeed;
And the masses of doubt that are floating about
Would smother a mortal creed.
But we that sit in a sturdy youth,
And still can drink strong ale,
Oh – let us put it away to infallible truth.
Which always shall prevail!

MONSIGNOR ROBERT HUGH BENSON

Father Martindale is to be trusted on this. His life puts before us a chain-smoking, novel-writing man of God, incapable of treachery.

THE clerical novelist is scarcely a latter-day phenomenon. Not only priests but Princes of the Church have turned to fiction. In the last century, both Newman and Wiseman wrote novels, as in this did Cardinal Spellman (*The Foundling*), though with somewhat less effect. One of the most gifted and energetic of priest story tellers was Monsignor Robert Hugh Benson.

Benson was born in 1871, his father was to become Archbishop of Canterbury and Hugh himself took Anglican Orders but eventually was drawn to the Roman Catholic Church. At first disdainful of Rome, he followed a route that had been charted earlier by Newman and the scores of converts who came in his wake. Newman and his fellows in the Oxford Movement sought to see the English Church as part of the Catholic Church, emphatically not a Protestant sect, but, for many, history and theology eroded this position until there was nothing left to do but turn to Rome. Half a century later, Robert Hugh Benson began with the same conviction about the Anglican Church as Catholic, but in his case too, gradually and painfully, he gave it up. He became a Roman Catholic in 1903 and was ordained a priest a year later, in Rome.

Any appreciation of Benson as a writer must take into account his devotional and apologetic works, but it can be said that the single motive of all his writing was to put the Roman Catholic faith compellingly before his reader.

Of his fiction, many, perhaps most, readers will prefer the historical novels which vividly evoke the England of the Reformation and the Recusants who sought to keep the old faith alive. *The King's Achievement* has stirred the pulse of generations of boys and girls and, thanks to the Neumann Press of Long Prairie, Minnesota, will continue to do so. *Come Wrack, Come Rope* was read avidly where I went to school, its popularity insured by that most effective of advertising, word of mouth.

One of Robert Hugh Benson's most amazing novels is *Lord of the World*, published in 1907; in it he takes on the ultimate subject, the end of the world. Projecting ahead to the year 2000, the novel presents a thoroughly secular society. The Enlightenment dream has been realized, a more or less benign humanism dominates, the final touches are put on a global government thanks to the charismatic efforts of a mysterious American named Julian Felsenburgh. At long last, man has taken control of his own destiny.

A first sign of this in the novel is the acceptance of euthanasia as the only sane and humane way to end not only illness but any despondency a person is unwilling to bear. But the genius of Benson is to depict as reasonable and humane a civilization that is the antithesis of Christianity. Of course some sort of religion is needed, and this is supplied by a civic cult of naturalistic pantheism. The whole thing is enormously plausible.

There is a Catholic remnant, and the pope, English as it happens, still resides in Rome. The fading tolerance for such a reminder of the past disappears when some London Catholics act against the pagan rites at which former priests officiate. Felsenburgh reacts by wiping out the English Catholics and reducing Rome to a pile of ashes. Out of these ashes arises the Church in its final phase.

Percy Franklin, an English cardinal, traveling between Rome and London at the time of the massacre, survives and is elected pope. With a small band he moves to the Holy Land. Julian Felsenburgh, it is now clear, is the Anti-Christ. The novel culminates in Armageddon.

It is a great read. Many readers were depressed by the novel, however, and Benson unwisely responded with another, *The Dawn of All*, which depicted the triumph of Catholicism in a near future. In every way it is a lesser book than *Lord of the World*. It is not just that, dramatically speaking, success is less interesting than failure, but the author clearly relishes the idea of a return to the Holy Roman Empire, with Augustine's two cities reconciled. The novel is in its way an instance of that "immanentizing of the eschaton" that characterizes the triumphant humanism of *Lord of the World*.

Robert Hugh Benson himself is an enigmatic figure. The Jesuit C. C. Martindale published a two-volume life of Benson in 1916, only two years after the death of the young monsignor at forty-three. An official biography, written under the eye of the subject's mother and brothers, it is nonetheless a fascinating and frank account. In Benson we do not find the intellectual acumen of a Newman nor the learned sophistication of a Ronald Knox. There is something superficial and freelance about him, something "enthusiastic." Once in the Church and ordained, he managed somehow to avoid most aspects of the priestly life. The pastoral role repelled him; he was simply no good at it. His preaching was acclaimed, though its theology was sometimes shaky. The writing of novels was for him a kind of extension of his preaching. The wonder is that so many of the novels are as good as they are. Taken all for all, Robert Hugh Benson is one of the most interesting turn-of-the-century converts.

It is plain that *Hadrian VII*, Frederick Rolfe's story of an English pope, influenced Benson when he wrote *Lord of the World*, different as the two novels are. Benson claimed to have read Rolfe's novel many times before he wrote to its author. He struck up a friendship with Rolfe – who styled himself Baron Corvo – with disastrous results. Befriending Corvo was always risky, but his vendetta against Benson was epic in its dimensions. This is a story in itself, to be taken up in another essay. Most of those who write on their friendship take the view that Benson treated Rolfe badly. But this is to accept as good money the word of Baron Corvo, a notorious counterfeiter of the truth. Father Martindale is to be trusted on this. His life puts before us a chain-smoking, novel-writing man of God, incapable of treachery.

Robert Hugh Benson wrote out of the ebullient confidence of his recovered Catholicism, addressing Catholics as fellow possessors of the truth and everyone else as potentially Catholic.

GEORGES BERNANOS

*Only by the recovery of the mystery of the human person,
and the sense of the profundity of freedom and human
destiny, can the trivialization of human existence be
overcome.*

Georges Bernanos was 38 years old when his first novel, *Under
the Sun of Satan*, was published in 1926. It is a remarkable novel
whose power is easily felt by the English reader in the Harry
Lorin Binsse translation that appeared in 1949. (An earlier, less
effective translation had appeared in 1940.) The prologue is a
chilling portrait of evil: The Story of Mouchette.

Mouchette is a sixteen-year-old girl who, when the story
opens, is pregnant by a womanizing marquis, a fact she denies to
her father, who nonetheless confronts the marquis and is laughed
out of the room. That night, Mouchette sneaks out and visits the
marquis, anxious to assure him that she did not tell her father.
The marquis is puzzled by this. Subtly, subtly, Bernanos opens
before us a girl who has chosen to be evil, not simply to act
wrongly. She lies, not to save herself or the marquis or herparents,
but in order to lie. The emotional mutations of this scene with
the marquis move plausibly and inexorably to Mouchette's shoot-
ing the marquis.

The next set scene presents Mouchette, now three months
pregnant, in a doctor's waiting room. We learn that she is now
having an affair with the doctor, whom she tries to convince that
he is the father of her child. He dismisses this, she doesn't press
it, and the scene becomes a cat-and-mouse game, in which the
girl toys with a frantic frightened middle-aged man whose wife is
upstairs.

No summary can possibly convey the skill with which Bernanos creates this portrait of gratuitous evil. What is the prologue a prologue to? To a portrait of sanctity, of a young country bumpkin priest modeled on the Curé d'Ars.

Moral failure is easier to imagine and to portray than virtue or heroism. Still, many artists have given us convincing, moving, ennobling portraits of heroism. But moral failure is not evil nor is heroism sanctity. Georges Bernanos, from the outset of his literary career, had an almost unique ability to provide his reader with an unforgettable sense of the stakes of life: good or evil, heaven or hell, God or Satan.

This first novel was not a fluke, a unique achievement. *Imposture* (1928), *Joy* (1929), and *Diary of a Country Priest* (1936) continue Bernanos's amazing performance. Hoping to make some money, he tried to write a murder mystery (*A Crime*), but he could not confine himself to the stylization of moral fault, as the genre may seem to require; inevitably, as it seems, the book was transformed into something far more, something profound, something that tapped the very wellsprings of human action.

Who was this man who in his late thirties commenced a literary career of such depth? After service in World War I, Georges Bernanos married and sold insurance in the provinces. Born in Paris, educated by the Jesuits, far right, a member of Action Française and indeed a royalist, he might have seemed an enthusiastic and doctrinaire young man. His war experience and then marriage tilted him in the direction of middle-class respectability. Wife, family, selling insurance – against that background, the novels surprise, even astound.

The truth is that from boyhood, Georges Bernanos's faith permeated his view of life. He was anti-democratic because he felt that modern political life trivialized the human agent, the free, intelligent person whose deeds and decisions in this life are decisive for eternity. His break with Action Française, his subsequent rejection of the Franco cause in Spain (*The Great Cemeteries under the Moon*), display a man who judged politics from a religious point of view, not vice versa.

Looked upon simply as a novelist, Bernanos's work can be seen as a corrective to the banality of much modern fiction. But it is a corrective taken in the name of the importance of the subject of fiction, namely, the responsible human agent with an eternal destiny.

In 1934, aged 46, after suffering an accident that left him lame, Bernanos moved with his family to Majorca in an effort to keep down expenses, and four years later he moved to South America, Paraguay briefly, then Brazil. Thus it was from exile that this quintessential Frenchmen, whose love of his country survived his disgust with and criticism of its moral and political tone, wrote the great non-fiction polemics which, added to his fiction, make him one of the greatest of French authors.

The Spanish Civil War presented many with a crossroads. Doctrinaire leftists and fellow travelers supported the Republic unquestioningly, a certain kind of Catholic blindly supported Franco. There were noble exceptions among French – and American – Catholics, and none more noble than Georges Bernanos. Living in Majorca, he had close-up experience of what was at issue. The late Thirties, the Second World War, swept Bernanos into a new role as a polemicist. Combative, prophetic, angry, Bernanos spoke from the heart to his countrymen throughout the war and the agony of occupation.

Asked by General De Gaulle, he returned to France in 1945, but he remained unclubbable. The Fourth Republic became the new target of his criticism. He was furious when it was proposed that he put himself forward for the French Academy. He avoided being honored by a society he considered corrupt, even after the crucible of its defeat and occupation.

Such a late work as *France against the Robots*, treating the mechanization of human life, can be read today for its perceptiveness. "A world dominated by power is an abominable world, but a world dominated by number is ignoble." In a society governed by polls, where self-knowledge and self-appraisal are sought through surveys and questionnaires, we are painfully aware of the quantification and false-objectification of human existence. Bernanos did not look to politics, now become the manipulation of citizens, for the remedy of modern ills. Only by the recovery of the mystery of the human person, and the sense of the profundity of freedom and human destiny, can the trivialization of human existence be overcome. Is there any wonder that Pope John Paul II came back again and again to the nature of the human person?

Bernanos foresaw what would happen when humans began to see themselves as robots, as machines responsive to extrinsic causes, their actions mere reactions. Nowadays even bishops speak of the misbehavior of the clergy, for example, as corrective by means of counseling, therapy, external causes. The concept of sin, of moral responsibility, has been weakened.

Shortly before he died, in 1948, in a letter to an old friend, Bernanos closed with a remark that sums up his vision of life. "May you feel the sweet presence of Jesus Christ who makes into one reality sorrow and joy, life and death." Bernanos was incapable of an unctuous remark or of pietism. He speaks here – he could not speak otherwise – out of the abundance of his heart. His novels give us Catholic fiction, not as an interesting subgenre, but as the only serious viewpoint from which the mystery of human existence can be imaginatively grasped.

ANTHONY BURGESS

His problem seems to have been the flesh rather than faith, the discomfort of confessing and the dread prospect of eternal punishment.

To the classical question, "What would you do if you were told you had a year to live?," Anthony Burgess responded with the resolution to write three or four novels, the income from which would cushion the loss to his widow.

The brain tumor that was supposed to kill him did not; it was his wife who died, and Anthony Burgess, once embarked on a literary career, never looked back until his death in 1993.

Although he published much, very much, it was Burgess's fate to be chiefly known for *A Clockwork Orange* – and that in its filmed form. He was also a musician, an expert on Shakespeare and Joyce. His was a capacious mind, messy, teeming with incoherence. He was also – this is not a conclusion from the above – uxorious. He married again and noted, late in his life, that he had no friends, just his wife.

His *nom de plume* takes the filling from the sandwich of his name, John Anthony Burgess Wilson. The Anthony was his confirmation name. The Catholicism of the Wilson family had survived from the persecution and ostracism that followed on the Reformation in England. Not that Wilson was an old Catholic in the manner of the denizens of Brideshead Hall.

Far from it. He came from humble surroundings and despite his formidable accomplishments always felt lower class and despised by the English elite. His exile from England was motivated in part by a desire to escape the confiscatory taxation of socialism, something which did not stop him from the usual snide remarks about Margaret Thatcher. But more basically, Burgess was driven by nostalgia for a Catholic Europe that no longer was.

His first wife was an Anglican, and during the marriage he drifted from the faith, though wanting to go back. His second wife was an anticlerical Italian, an atheist. Burgess seems to have been ruled by his wives in religious matters. Kingsley Amis in his *Memoirs* has a chapter on Burgess in which both wives, Lynne and Liana, are cattily skewered by an Amis who seems genuinely to have liked Burgess despite his "frightening fecundity."

Was Burgess a Catholic? Certainly not a practicing one. Did he disbelieve? Perhaps, but he did not have the courage of his lack of conviction. "I took the opportunity, while Liana was sleeping, to baptize Paolo Andrea in rain-water: *Ego te baptizo Paulum* – did Andrea take a Latin or Greek accusative? – *in nomine Patris et Filii et Spiritus Sancti, Amen*. At need any layman was permitted to do it. It was best to be on the safe side."

This is from the second volume of his autobiography, in which one continues to come upon reminders of Burgess's not quite lost faith. The linguistic allusion in the midst of this furtive liturgy rings true. Burgess's *A Mouthful of Air* is a fascinating and quite scholarly study of language. Of course he invented a language for *A Clockwork Orange*. In part it was his fascination with that old language teacher, James Joyce, another exile from faith and fatherland, who eventually wrote, as one might say, Indo-European. Burgess's book on the Irish author is called *Re Joyce*.

Burgess's literary career began with a trilogy set in Malaya which has many good things in it, but is after all an instance of its genre, the British colonial novel, though it is savingly Orwellian and Greenian in its outlook. It was after this that Burgess got the unnerving news that the tumor on his brain would kill him within a year. The novels he desperately wrote for motives already stated show signs of hasty composition.

He had been warned off an earlier novel which, he tells us, arose out of a "phase of Catholic guilt" promoted by reading

Graham Greene's *The Heart of the Matter*. "I am still capable of moaning and breast-beating at my defection from, as I recognize, the only system that makes spiritual and intellectual sense. But I see that the novel, an essentially comic and Protestant art-form, is no place for the naked posturing of religious guilt." An odd remark, coming after the mention of Greene's masterful story of religious guilt.

As a serious and professional writer, Burgess was amused by the effortless nonsense that was thought to express "creativity." He knew the difficulty of writing well. "We need some Johnsonian or Ruskinian pundit to frighten everybody with near impossible conditions for true creativity. We have to stop thinking that what kindergarten children produce with pencil or watercolor, is anything more than charming or quaint. If you want to be considered a poet, you will have to show mastery of the Petrarchan sonnet form or the sestina. Your musical efforts must begin with well-formed fugues. There is no substitute for craft."

There is no one, I imagine, who has read all of Burgess now that he is dead, except perhaps his second wife Liana. He published over thirty novels, as many volumes of non-fiction, he wrote for children, he was a poet and also a translator. He was a man of letters who lived by his pen. His pen was mightier than his sorrow, driving away the sense of being lower class, not accepted by Oxbridge intellectuals, salving somewhat, perhaps, his ambiguous attitude toward the faith.

"I say that I lost my faith, but really I was no more than a lapsed Catholic, as boring a figure as the stage Irishman and sometimes the same figure. What makes him a bore is his lachrymosity, especially in drink, about being a bad son who has struck his mother and dare not go home."

He occupies this role fitfully in giving us a narrative version of his life. The first volume of his autobiography is called *Little Wilson and Big God*. His problem seems to have been the flesh rather than faith, the discomfort of confessing and the dread prospect of eternal punishment. "The rage I wake to and take to bed is a turbulence not always related to an object." This is from the epilogue to the autobiography.

Burgess was a regular on television where he paraded eccentricities and a kind of schoolyard, though erudite, naughtiness about sexual matters. He points out that a reason Catholicism retained its hold on him is that it contains a philosophical as well as a theological system. In that philosophical base is the common morality of mankind. Why remorse as moral failure should be called religious guilt is not wholly clear. It was hell that haunted Burgess, death and hell. They amount to half of the Four Last Things so one wants to think that he spent a lifetime pondering the end.

Theologians write, with studied ambiguity, of anonymous Christians. Sociologists speak of ethnic Catholics as if faith, like freckles, is willy-nilly with you till the end. Nonetheless, it is certain that there are some authors who have lapsed and yet go on being Catholic in their imaginative fix on the world. The driven, daunting, diverting, polytalented Anthony Burgess was one of them. He is often in my prayers. I commend him to yours, along with his books.

WILLA CATHER

"The church looked powerful and triumphant there on its eminence, so high above the rest of the landscape, with miles of warm color lying at its feet . . ."

HAS anyone ever written about the way Catholicism enters into the work of non-Catholic writers? I am sure this has been done, at least in a piece-meal fashion. In reading the Brontës or Thackeray or Dickens or Trollope one notices the odd way Catholics and things Catholic are treated. Recently Robert Fussel wrote *The Catholic Side of Henry James*, a remarkable study that traces the way the Church attracts and repels James's characters.

A bonus of reading this book was learning that Ralph Waldo Emerson had a habit of visiting the old cathedral of Baltimore when he was in that city. Surely this is one of the most American of Catholic churches, architecturally speaking, but it was the difference rather than the similarity that interested Emerson, and his eye was on the service. He wrote his wife that it was such a relief to see a ceremony in which the preacher was not the star.

Surely such a book could be done on Howells and Hawthorne as well, since it was often the European experience that unsettled the native American. At home, the American Protestant might think of Romanism as a foreign and exotic business, but in Europe he was forced to see that it was he who was outside the dominant culture and religion. The role that Dante played in altering the attitude of Yankee Protestants toward the "old religion" is well known.

In this century, Willa Cather (1873–1947) is a non-Catholic author whose attitude toward Catholicism moves from the untroubled tolerance of *O Pioneers!* to the empathetic treatments of *Death Comes for the Archbishop* and *Shadows on the Rock*. Born in Virginia, raised in Nebraska, an editor first in Pittsburgh, then New York, Cather visited Europe, returned to Nebraska annually, loved the Southwestern United States, and vacationed in Maine and New Brunswick. She is one of the great American novelists of the 20th century.

Alexandra is the dominant figure in *O Pioneers!*, her father's daughter, who after his death manages his prairie farm with remarkable success. A casualty of her filial devotion is her love for her childhood friend Carl. The hinge event of the novel is a double murder when Alexandra's brother Emil is caught *in flagrante delicto* with the Catholic Frank Shabata's wife, Marie. The novel has an elegiac tone, set by the invocation of Whitman in the title, with Alexandra providing a wise daughter of the soil's outlook on events. She and the reader are awestruck by the mystery of human freedom as it plays out against the inexorable rhythms of the land.

The French parish of Sainte-Agnes to which the Shabatas belong is an integral part of the Nebraska setting. "The church looked powerful and triumphant there on its eminence, so high above the rest of the landscape, with miles of warm color lying at its feet, and by its position and setting it reminded one of some of the churches built long ago in the wheat-lands of middle France." Sometimes Alexandra goes to Catholic services with Marie Shabata, and a parish fair that all the main characters, Protestant and Catholic attend, provides a background for one sequence. The reader is confident Cather is describing something she herself has seen.

This confidence is strengthened when we consider her description of the bishop's visit to confirm. The men ride out to meet him. "Five miles east of Sainte-Agnes they met the bishop in his open carriage, attended by two priests. Like one man the boys swung off their hats in a broad salute, and bowed their heads as the handsome old man lifted his two fingers in the episcopal blessing." She doesn't get that quite right – the thumb and index finger touch with three fingers extended – but one notices the desire for accuracy.

I think this is the first bishop to appear in Cather's fiction. Soon she will go on from the external glimpse to imaginatively occupying the inside of Catholic prelates with extraordinary effect. *Death Comes for the Archbishop*, based on Archbishop Lamy of Santa Fe, was written when Cather's artistic skills were honed and when her distinctive outlook was formed. It is instructive to compare Paul Horgan's life of Lamy with Cather's artistic use of the archbishop in this novel. Cather's love and knowledge of the Southwest is everywhere evident in the novel, but one is amazed by her treatment and understanding of her hero. The final lines of the novel give a sense of the portrait she has drawn.

> When the Cathedral bell tolled just after dark, the Mexican population of Santa Fe fell upon their knees, and all American Catholics as well. Many others who did not kneel prayed in their hearts. Eusabio and the Tesuque brothers went quietly away to tell their people; and the next morning the old Archbishop lay before the high altar in the church he had built.

The historical novel Willa Cather wrote of Quebec had as its principal literary sources the histories of Francis Parkman and the *Jesuit Relations*. Parkman's rationalist anti-clericalism had no effect on Cather, and she rejected entirely his negative estimate of Bishop Laval, influenced perhaps by her conversations with the vicar of Ste-Foy, Abbé Scott. She read too the letters of Marie de l'Incarnation, from one of which she took the motto of the novel. Describing the flowers of the region to a sister in France, the nun generalizes: "Tout y est suavage, les fleurs aussi bien que les hommes: Here everything is wild, the flowers as well as the men."

In *Shadows on the Rock*, Cather writes of 17th-century French Canada and of two forceful men, Count Frontenac and Bishop

Laval. But the story is told through lesser characters and in a sense the rocky promontory on which Quebec stands is the subject insofar as it symbolizes the "narrow but definite" culture the French established there.

Sometimes writers choose their subjects, as often as not the reverse is true. *Death Comes for the Archbishop* grew gradually from Cather's visits and study of the southwest; *Shadows on the Rock* was worked up on the basis of less personal experience. In either case, we can be surprised that such characters and events appealed to a non-Catholic author. Cather's authorial voice owes much to Scripture. Her acceptance of the misfortunes and follies of men depended upon seeing life whole and catching an intimation of its deeper purpose.

In *O Pioneers!*, Alexandra takes a long train ride to the prison in which Frank Shabata is paying for killing her brother and Marie Shabata. This is done matter-of-factly, but it is clearly the kind of thing Willa Cather expects a Christian like Alexandra Bergson to do. It is no wonder that an author capable of finding nobility in the simple could also find the common clay in the mighty.

WILLA CATHER'S CATHOLIC NOVELS

Among the imaginary conversations I would like to overhear, one between Willa Cather and biographers claiming her for feminism, even sexual aberration, would rank high on the list. As with Kate Chopin, she is often subjected to an ideological reading that misses not only the high artistry of her work but also its sane serenity.

She was a church-going believer all her life; she was confirmed in the Episcopal Church, along with her parents, on December 27, 1922, by the Bishop of Nebraska, a family friend. Even her slightest works convey a sense of life completely different from that of those angry females who presume to speak for their sisters. But this correction does little to solve one of the great mysteries about Willa Cather. How was she able to write two of the most Catholic novels in American literature?

Death Comes for the Archbishop first appeared in 1927 when Cather was fifty-four. The novel had been forming in the author's imagination for over a dozen years, triggered by her reaction to the Catholic history and artifacts of the American Southwest during frequent visits.

> The more I stayed in the Southwest, the more I felt that the story of the Catholic Church in that country was the most interesting of all its stories. The old mission churches, even those which were abandoned and in ruins, had a moving reality about them; the hand-carved beams and joists, the utterly unconventional frescoes, the countless fanciful figures of the saints, not two of them alike, seemed a deeper expression of some very real and lively human feeling.

Cather's roots were in Virginia, but her family had moved to Nebraska when she was ten years old, and it was on the prairie that her imagination was formed. The pioneers, coming as they did from a variety of countries, provided a corrective for the received vision of America as merely an extension of the Puritan colonies. When Cather encountered the Catholicism of the Southwest, she had already written of European Catholics emigrating to the New World. In the early novels, Catholics are not presented as Americans *manqués*; their difference is due to their eastern European origins rather than their faith.

The bronze statue of Archbishop Lamy in front of the cathedral in Santa Fe fascinated Cather, and the archbishop became "a sort of invisible personal friend" in her vacation wanderings through the Southwest. He had come, a well-bred, distinguished Frenchman, as bishop into a land whose Catholicism had Spanish roots. Lamy was a 19th-century version of those Spanish priests who had arrived in the desert to evangelize the natives and to create the little pockets of civilization that are still there for the viewing. The missionary bishop Lamy arrived in a land where vestiges of a vast earlier missionary effort were all around him and prior to that had been the culture and religion of the natives. How old the New World was.

Who has not marveled at the Spanish missions, in California, in New Mexico, in Texas? In Albuquerque one stands before a church that shatters the notion that American history has its roots only in New England. Willa Cather might have seemed a perfect recruit to the WASP ascendancy. When she went east, she was soon at home in the worlds of art and publishing. But some inner need took her back to Red Cloud, Nebraska, year after year, and on camping trips to remote parts of the country, an impulse that brought her eventually to the Southwest and the layered Catholic history of that country extending back over centuries.

When Mortimer Adler became a fervent advocate of Thomas Aquinas, he was regularly asked if he intended to become a Catholic. He replied by quoting the *Summa theologiae*: faith is a grace and a gift. So when *Death Comes for the Archbishop* appeared, similar questions must have arisen about its author. The editors of *Commonweal* asked her about it, and she replied with a letter of essay length. In the three-volume Library of America edition of her works, this essay appears twice, once in the notes to the novel and a second time in the volume called *Stories, Poems, and Other Writings*.

One is struck by two things in this essay. First, speaking in her own name, Cather conveys the same matter-of-fact sympathy with Catholicism and its history that permitted the artistic adoption of that outlook in the novel. Neither in this novel, nor in the next, *Shadows on the Rock*, is there any distance at all between the author and her characters. There is never the sense that things are being viewed with an alien, albeit friendly, eye. Second, there are precious remarks about the method she employed in the novel, a method that would be employed as well in *Shadows on the Rock*.

> I had all my life wanted to do something in the style
> of legend, which is absolutely the reverse of dramatic

treatment. Since I first saw the Puvis de Chavannes frescoes of the life of Saint Genevieve in my student days, I have wished that I could try something like that in prose; something without accent, with none of the artificial elements of composition.

This method seems peculiarly apt for the novel she undertook. "The essence of such writing is not to hold the note, not to use an incident for all there is in it – but to touch and pass on." She had come upon a life of Father Joseph Machebeuf, an associate of Lamy's and eventual first bishop of Denver, written by a Father William Joseph Howlett and printed, as she put it, on a country press at Pueblo, Colorado. The book was thick with letters the priest had written to his sister Philomene, and Cather found in these letters "the mood, the spirit in which they accepted the accidents and hardships of a desert country, the joyful energy that kept them going."

It is easy to imagine someone else coming upon such a book and setting it aside with a smile. A little amateur hagiography, published in the sticks since it could not possibly interest a "real" publisher. For Cather it was a priceless source of the spirit of the missionary, his trust in providence, his holiness. In her Catholic novels, it is the simple holiness of the main characters that is conveyed with authority. It seems demeaning to refer to those letters home of a missionary priest as Willa Cather's principal "research" for her novel. She tells us that she deliberately avoided steeping herself in Catholic lore, but when she needed advice she sought it from Father Dennis Fitzgerald in Red Cloud, Nebraska, who had studied in Rome. But she set aside most of what he told her: it was not the furnishings of the faith but its essence that she was after.

Shadows on the Rock shifts from the American Southwest to Quebec. Francis Parkman had written of these matters in a series of works that fill two chubby volumes in the Library of America. We are told that Willa Cather began to reread Parkman in 1928 during a visit to Quebec, where she also met Father Henri Arthur Scott, a Canadian church historian.

I am sure that someone has studied the contrast between the outlook of the historian Parkman and the novelist Willa Cather toward the French Catholic culture of Quebec. I think it fair to say that, for all his industry and amazing comprehensiveness, there remains a barrier between Parkman and his subject matter. Parkman was a Protestant, the son of a Boston minister, who had felt the lure of Catholicism that Henry James spoke of, but had danced out of danger. The fascination continued, but it was a wary curiosity. Toward the end of his life, he became a foe of feminism and women's suffrage and campaigned against parochial schools as dangerous competition to public schools. His anti-clericalism proved an impediment to his receiving an honorary doctorate from my *alma mater*, Laval University. Willa Cather, on the other hand, enters the world of her Catholic characters in *Death Comes for the Archbishop* and *Shadows on the Rock* and tells their story in such a way that there is no authorial otherness at all.

As with the earlier novel, so here some of her characters are based on historical figures. *Death Comes for the Archbishop* covers a lifetime; *Shadows on the Rock* covers a year, the interval between the sailing of the last ship in the fall to the arrival of the first ship from France in the spring. Monsignor Laval is a major figure but we see him as we see everyone else-through the eyes of the pharmacist's daughter, Cecile. It is hard not to see her as the girl Willa Cather had been, and this makes the adoption of the simple Catholic piety of the girl all the more moving.

Brian Moore, an excellent novelist, published *Black Robe* a few years ago, a novel of a Canadian missionary. Comparison of the artistic achievements of this novel and Willa Cather's *Shadows on the Rock* would take one very far afield. Moore was raised Catholic, and his story is manifestly a sort of Graham Greene inside/outside reenactment. In *Catholics* Moore created the haunting character of an abbot who had lost his faith yet held his community together. Cather is interested in the firm and unwavering faith of the archbishop and of Marchebeuf. There are irregular clergy on the scene, priests with concubines, gourmands, but her method of "not holding the note," of touching and passing on, does not give them equal billing. Indeed, they are seen through the eyes of the faithful priest who is living out the promises of his youth.

A poignant note in Cather's letter to *Commonweal* is struck when she notes that "newer priests down in that country have been taking away from those old churches their old homely images and decorations, which have a definite artistic and historic value, and replacing them by conventional, factory-made furnishings from New York. It is a great pity." Indeed it is.

Those of us who have lived through even more egregious dismantling, carried on in the mistaken belief that it was a response to Vatican II, can only agree. The language, the place, the reverence of the liturgy have been reduced to a point where the Mass seems only a meeting like a dozen others. It is not nostalgia that is at issue. There may be an English equivalent of the gravity of Latin; there may be another music that engages the mind and heart in the way that Gregorian chant does; there may be churches that can match the achievements of an earlier day. But they will have to arise out of the same vibrant and simple faith that produced their counterparts. Now cardinals commission agnostics to design cathedrals, tinkling pianos and ill-plucked guitars fill the churches, and translators with tin ears twist the liturgy into conformity with alien ideologies. Willa Cather became Archbishop Latour and Cecile, but this was more than an artistic achievement. She shared their Christian faith and aspiration to holiness. The faith that moves mountains also builds cathedrals, finds the right music, inspires a language appropriate to its aspirations. And it produces novels like *Death Comes for the Archbishop* and *Shadows on the Rock*.

GILBERT KEITH CHESTERTON

*Father Brown never meets a criminal he could not himself be,
and it is that which enables him to see what others overlook.*

A PARADOX is not a couple of mallards but a statement seemingly,
but only seemingly, in conflict with itself. The paradox is the
note of Chesterton's style as well as the subject of Hugh Kenner's
book on the English author. Almost any page of Chesterton will
yield examples.

> The mad man has not lost his reason; he has lost every-
> thing but his reason.
>
> He is the man of whom men say that he means well;
> by which they mean that he means nothing.
>
> Women were not kept at home to keep them narrow;
> on the contrary, they were kept at home to keep them
> broad.

And of course it was Chesterton who noted of the claim that no
one can turn the clock back that of course anyone can, and with
one finger.

This feature of Chesterton's prose endears him to many and
puts off others, but it would be wrong to see it simply as a matter
of style. Chesterton was the great *naif*, for whom the everyday
was shot through with mystery and romance. His best stories
evoke the wonder and surprise of the ordinary. Thus he will write
of a *Napoleon of Notting Hill* and a *Man who was Thursday*. He himself was a man who was thirsty, and celebrated the Christian
blessing of drink with something of the exuberance of his friend
Hilaire Belloc, and the occasional immoderation of a son of
Adam.

The paradox of Chesterton is that of a man who spent his life pouring out evanescent writing, aimed at dailies and weeklies, showing little or no concern for any future reputation, yet whose swift journalism now reads like the studied essays of others. He was a master of the personal essay which often functioned as little more than a journalistic filler, and yet, when collected, these have an undeniable permanency. Essays were usually *on* something, but like Belloc Chesterton could dash off an essay on little or nothing, yet in the course of it, some gemlike truth would emerge, show this overlooked facet or that, and prevent the piece from simply going the way of old newsprint.

Ignatius Press is bringing out Chesterton's Collected Works, and this is a genuine initiative, there never having been such a thing before. Quite rightly the editors have devoted whole volumes to Chesterton's journalism. There is a hurried helter-skelter aspect to the things Chesterton composed as books. *Orthodoxy*, one of his most intellectually exciting books, was more or less dashed off, as was his remarkable book on Thomas Aquinas. If we can trust the accounts of the composition of this latter work, Chesterton sounds like an utterly irresponsible writer. He had read little of St. Thomas, and he dictated half the book before he asked his secretary to get him some books on the saint. He leafed through these, and dictated the rest of the book. The result is a grasp of the central effort of Thomas's intellectual life expressed in a way that has excited the envy of such scholars as Etienne Gilson.

In his literary appreciations, quoting from memory, like a medieval, Chesterton often remembers lines that his author never wrote, or gets them slightly wrong – and thereby gets them right in a way that surpasses mere accuracy. Writing on Chaucer or Dickens or the Victorian Age in Literature, Chesterton writes of authors he has read and loved for readers he assumes have done the same. He addresses the *aficionado*, not the expert. The point of his literary criticism is to enhance our future re-reading, to take us back to the author, not to produce something that could exist apart from what it is about.

> Whatever the word "great" means, Dickens was what it means. Even the fastidious and unhappy who cannot read his books without a continuous critical exasperation, would use the word of him without stopping to think. They feel that Dickens is a great writer even if he is not a good writer. . . . "Great" is the first adjective which even the most supercilious modern critic would apply to Dickens. And "great" is the last adjective the most supercilious critic would apply to himself. We do not dare to be great men, even when we claim to be superior to them.

A book that starts like that is going to be read, and it was read and it is read. And its point is to get us to read Dickens.

Chesterton's poetry has the unassuming character of an effusion from a multi-talented man who could not not write. It is uneven – his output generally is uneven – but it has moments of exquisite beauty. Perhaps all poets are fated to be remembered for a few lines, a few poems, their *oeuvre* sinking out of sight. Chesterton's "Lepanto" and his "Ballad of St. Barbara" will surely last.

It is altogether fitting that Chesterton is most known to most today through his Father Brown stories. They have never gone out of print; they have been translated into films and into a television series. They belong to a genre and yet are *sui generis*. It may not be true that Charlie Chaplin once entered a Charlie Chaplin look-alike contest, and came in third. But it is certainly true that any tyro could write a technically tighter detective story than any of the Father Brown stories.

What characterizes them is their sense of the mystery and unpredictability of human freedom as well as an awareness of a nature wounded by sin. Father Brown never meets a criminal he could not himself be, and it is that which enables him to see what others overlook. There is a great contrast between Sherlock Holmes and Father Brown – indeed, Chesterton's priest seems devised to show the unreality of a rationalist deductive approach to human doings. In "The Man with Two Beards," Chesterton contrasted a rational, and false, interpretation of what happened, with a fantastic and true one.

What Doyle and Chesterton had in common, perhaps, was a loss of interest in their own character. Doyle notoriously tried to do away with Sherlock so that he could devote himself more to his wholly forgotten other literary efforts. The Father Brown stories seem to fade as we move away from the first collection, though each of the four collections contains gems. These stories were merely one of the many things Chesterton wrote.

Along with *Orthodoxy*, *The Everlasting Man* seems certain to be read for pleasure and profit by generations to come. Biographies of Chesterton appear regularly now. As a man he was a puzzler. He wrote about his conversion years before coming into the Church. He shared with Belloc views nowadays considered politically incorrect. But he knew the English were wrong in Ireland and wrong in South Africa and that the "liberation" of women would enslave them. He dreamt of an economic system – Distributivism – between Socialism and Capitalism. He wrote English like an angel.

KATE CHOPIN

*It has been said that great fiction does not so much produce
an effect as an after-effect, a lingering meditative mood that
alters however mildly our sensibility.*

SHE was born in Saint Louis in 1850 as Kate O'Flaherty, three-quarters Irish, but the remaining fourth was the imaginatively dominant element. Her Creole grandmother lived with the family in Saint Louis and exercised a great influence on Kate. The dominance of the Creole in her mind and imagination was sealed when she married Oscar Chopin in 1870 and was taken off to New Orleans by her husband, where they lived for nine years, during which Kate had five sons. When Oscar met with hard times as a cotton broker, they moved to his family's property in Natchitoches Parish. Ensconced in Cloutierville, Kate had a daughter, and it was there, in 1882, that Oscar died of malaria. In 1884, she returned with her family to Saint Louis.

When eventually she began to write, those fourteen years in Louisiana, particularly the three years in Cloutierville, provided the country of her imagination. She began writing short stories around 1890, using Creole settings and often the *patois* of her characters. Her writing career came to an end when her third novel *The Awakening* so shocked some readers that it was removed from the Saint Louis library and Kate was roundly condemned far and wide.

This is the woman who in recent years has been taken up by feminists and depicted as a celebrant of unbridled female passion and a woman's right to enjoy her body, etc., etc. Almost all recent commentary on Kate Chopin anachronistically enlists her in the gender wars. What did earlier readers make of her?

By and large, she wasn't read much. In 1941, a dissertation was written at Notre Dame, under the direction of the legendary Frank O'Malley, and there is an earlier important book by Daniel S. Rankin, *Kate Chopin and Her Creole Stories* that appeared in 1932. Given the spin that has recently been put on her work, it is interesting to see what earlier critics had to say about this remarkable woman and her literary career, which lasted approximately ten years, from 1889 to 1899, when her controversial last novel appeared.

Like Willa Cather, Chopin often puts before the reader strong female characters. The influence of her grandmother and her own effort to continue running her husband's store after his death, gave her a practical sense of what a woman can do. But this is scarcely the only theme of her writing.

"Odalie Misses Mass" is a delightful little tale of a young girl's sitting with the senile Aunt Pinky while the others go off to Mass. The old Black woman, who had given her life to the family, murmurs to the girl that those she cared for do not visit her now. "Don' fret, Aunt Pinky – I'm goin' – to stay with – you." "No pussun nuva come back 'cep' you." The girl nods off and when she wakes the old woman is dead. Typically, Chopin lets the story speak for itself; no moral is drawn.

In such Creole stories, Kate Chopin puts vividly before the reader a vignette that means much more than it says. It has been said that great fiction does not so much produce an effect as an after-effect, a lingering meditative mood that alters however mildly our sensibility. With many of the Creole stories, Kate Chopin produces such an after-effect.

Stories like "At the 'Cadian Ball" and "The Storm," called a sequel to the former, prefigure the novel *The Awakening*. The sequel presents an adulterous interlude between Alcée and Calixta. The incident is told with frank detail, and there are no consequences which diminish Calixta's acceptance of this moment of pleasure. Alcée writes reassuringly to his absent wife, telling her there is no need to hurry home, and the story ends with the wife reading the letter and reflecting that she can forego their intimate conjugal life for a time. "So the storm passed and everyone was happy."

It was Kate Chopin's presentation of a woman indulging her passions with impunity that caught the eye of feminists, some of whom seem to think that this had never before been done in fiction, forgetful apparently of the Brontës. Is it fair to this writer to see her as giving us "the exultation of passion in the dark heart of the wilderness?"

If "The Storm" leaves its sinners overtly unpunished, the same can hardly be said for the novel that elicited such a negative reaction. In *The Awakening*, Edna, a Presbyterian, marries a Creole Catholic, Leonce Pontellier, whose treatment of her is correct but empty, and her sense of dissatisfaction is given shape when she falls in love with Robert who, however, soon goes away. She then engages in a purely sensual affair with Alcée, which leaves her even more dissatisfied. Robert returns, she declares her love to him, and, in the midst of the declaration, she is called away to assist at a birth. She ponders the claim of her children and her love for Robert, only to find that he has not awaited her return. His note reads, "Good-by – because I love you." She then commits suicide by swimming out to sea until her strength gives out. The novel ends with her aware of sounds from shore. The end. No comment.

Kate Chopin was stunned by the shocked reaction to her novel. In a humorous response, she suggested that she had no idea Edna would make such a mess of things – "working out her own damnation as she did" – but by the time she realized it, the story was half done.

Rankin sees the influence of D'Anunzio and the morbidity of the *fin de siècle* on the novel he calls "exotic in setting, morbid in theme, erotic in motivation."

Somewhere between this estimate and the feminist assumption that she means to glorify passion may lie the real truth about Kate Chopin. She was after all a Catholic who saw her heroine as damned. To show the plausibility of adultery and its fleeting attractions is hardly questionable. In many ways the novel prefigures Greene's *Heart of the Matter*. The feminist critic imagines that Chopin gives us in the heroine of *The Awakening* a model of female behavior, that the woman who betrays her husband and children, her lover and herself, is somehow the better for it. Surely it is libelous to attribute such nonsense to Kate O'Flaherty Chopin.

PAUL CLAUDEL

But it was not until he was seventy eight that this ferocious Catholic was elected to the French Academy.

THERE is a marker set in the floor of Notre Dame, near one of the great pillars in the choir, which commemorates the return to the faith of Paul Claudel. *Ici se convertit Paul Claudel.* His conversion, as he called it, took place on Christmas Eve. He was eighteen at the time, and his drift from the faith had not been due to the temptations flesh is heir to, particularly in the teens. Rather, it was the free-thinking atmosphere of the intellectual milieu in which he was educated that led him astray. A school prize he won was awarded by Ernest Renan, the self-important apostate whose life of Jesus was an early entry in the "demythologization" of Christianity and was a marked influence on the times.

Claudel did not return immediately to the practice of his faith. But on that Christmas Eve in Notre Dame, the liturgy spoke to him with a power he would never forget, and his disbelief drained from him.

Claudel was a triple threat – a poet of oceanic force; a playwright whose works transformed a secularized theater with the drama of salvation; an art critic.

Paul Claudel entered the French diplomatic service as a very young man and through a long career was stationed in increasingly important posts around the world. Born in 1868, his conversion took place on December 25, 1886; in 1893 he was posted to the United States for a year in the French consulates in New York and Boston. Next were posts in China but, in 1900, returned to France, he spent some time in a Benedictine monastery testing a vocation he decided was not his. So it was back to China and an event whose full dimensions have become known only in recent years.

Claudel had an affair with a married woman whose husband's business interest it was his task as consul to further. The liaison became a local scandal, and Paris was informed. The woman, Rose Vetch, returned to Europe alone and, as it transpired, pregnant with Claudel's child. In Belgium she entered into another liaison, and disappeared from Claudel's life. He sought her desperately and for a six-month period turned away from the faith, even contemplating suicide. It was not until thirteen years later, on the occasion of their daughter's first communion, that he heard from Rose. By that time, Claudel had married and was the father of four children.

Le Partage du Midi (Break of Noon) is the play in which Claudel made use of this tragic and passionate encounter. As it had with St. Augustine, Claudel's sin and its attendant humiliation was the making of him spiritually.

His diplomatic career included assignments as French Ambassador to Japan, to the United States, to Belgium. When he retired in 1935, at the age of sixty seven, he had twenty more years to live. But it was not until he was seventy eight that this ferocious Catholic was elected to the French Academy.

The Tidings Brought to Mary; the play devoted to Christopher Columbus; the great Trilogy consisting of *The Hostage, Stale Bread*, and *The Humiliated Father* in which Claudel looks at the modern world through the eyes of faith – these assure his fame.

His letters make clear that he was ever on the *qui vive* for those who might be interested in the faith – his long correspondence with André Gide record a failed effort. Anne Delbée's *Une Femme*, the life of Paul's sister Camille, a sculptress who was the mistress of Rodin, has been made into a movie (*Camille*) in which Paul is portrayed as a prissy and pietistic figure. This is historically false. When Camille became the mistress of Rodin, Paul was caught up in his own adulterous affair. Camille spent the last thirty years of her life in an asylum, driven mad by Rodin, smashing her own statues about which Paul had written so eloquently. By the time Camille was confined, in 1913, Paul's life was back on track. Small wonder that he should have sought to extricate his sister from a demeaning, destructive, and sinful situation.

Claudel's *Five Great Odes* show the influence of Scripture on his poetry. It turns out that the Bible was his lifelong passion. The Vulgate was always on his desk, and his journal is almost a florilegium of Latin verses. *I Love the Bible* – as *J'aime la Bible* would be called if it were translated – is a good introduction to Claudel on Scripture.

He was a vocal foe of the new trends in biblical scholarship, deploring the work of Father Lagrange and the *école biblique* he opened in Jerusalem. While it is difficult to agree with Claudel on this, it is impossible not to sympathize with him. In some respects, his is an argument from the literary genres employed in the sacred texts. Who can understand the poetry of the Old Testament except a man who understands poetry, preeminently the poet himself. To subject the text to a disengaged dissection is not to get to the heart of it but to eviscerate it.

Nearly a third, ten volumes, of Claudel's *Oeuvres Complètes* are devoted to his reading of Scripture. These volumes are the fruit of a lifetime spent reading the text, as a form of prayer, as the act of a believer. None of this work has been translated. I am not sure how much of it is even read. I once asked a biblicist what the estimation of Claudel's scriptural writings was. I drew a total blank. But an establishment that keeps Claude Tresmontant at arms length is hardly ready for Paul Claudel.

It was my great good fortune years ago to be given by my wife Claudel's *Journal* in the two volumes of the Bibliothèque de la Pleiade. What a privilege to listen in as this man of enormous faith comments on Scripture, broods over his faults, offers up the boredom of the diplomatic life, engages in polemics and poetic flights, edifies.

Claudel died in 1955, a patriarchal figure, one of the official immortals of French literature, to the end a daily communicant.

"... Je vois l'eglise ouverte. Il faut entrer.
Mère de Jésus-Christ, je ne viens pas prier.
Je n'ai rien à offrir et rien à demander.
Je viens seulement, Mère, pour vous regarder."

(Finding the church open, I must go in./ Mother of Jesus, I am not come to pray./ I have nothing to offer, nothing to ask./ Mother, I have come only to see you.)

Lines from *La Vierge à Midi*. Paul Claudel was buried from Notre Dame, the cathedral in which all those years before he had turned again to God.

In 1993 Gilles Cornec published *L'affaire Claudel*, a book that considers the reasons why Claudel continues to be hated by so many of his countrymen. That a man might be at once poet, diplomat, and Catholic is an affront to those for whom art is necessarily a rejection of the common demands of human life, an end in itself, a substitute for religion. The poet's grave was desecrated in 1980. Perhaps one should see in this a proof of how seriously the French take their artists. Claudel took his art seriously by seeing it as his vocation, or perhaps it would be better to say that he saw it in terms of the one vocation that embraced his poetic production, his diplomatic profession, and his family. There are writers, already loved and hated by many, whose greatness seems still largely unplumbed. Claudel is one of them.

BARON CORVO

He ran out of funds, he ran out of friends, he ran out of everything but an almost total self-absorption.

IMPOVERISHED, paranoid, sexually perverted, raging against the world, a sad figure of a man died in Venice in 1912 at the age of fifty two. He had failed at every career he undertook, priest, photographer – artist, novelist, gondolier, pornographer – by any reckoning the waters of the lagoon should have closed over him and total oblivion claimed him. Not at all. He has been the subject of nearly a dozen books, writers from all points of the cultural spectrum – Graham Greene, W. H. Auden, Pamela Hansford Johnson – have written of him, a play based on his best novel had a Broadway run a few years ago. Nothing succeeds like failure.

Frederick Rolfe came into the Church in his late twenties and despite his age became a student for the priesthood, but he was dropped after a year. Another bishop took him up, and he was sent to the Scots College in Rome. This time he lasted less than a year before being expelled, literally – his bed with him still in it was taken out onto the street and left there.

But if the man was thus taken out of the seminary, the seminary was never taken out of the man. He came to style himself Baron Corvo, a wholly bogus title, but his abiding image of himself was as the priest he never was. The most often reprinted photograph of Rolfe shows him in biretta, cassock, Roman collar, and cloak. This priest manqué avenged himself on reality with an extraordinary novel, *Hadrian VII*, the story of an English pope who is none other than Frederick Rolfe under the name of George Arthur Rose.

In every genre there are unfinished works which are cherished more than most completed ones. There are unfinished symphonies, there are the Pensées of Pascal, notes for the great apologetic work he never wrote, there is the *Summa theologiae* of Thomas Aquinas. Analogously, there are works that survive only in fragments but are nonetheless ranked among the greatest, like Aristotle's *Poetics* and the poems of Sappho. Failed artists, like prodigals, are often preferred in somewhat the same way uncompleted masterworks are.

The fame of Rimbaud and F. Scott Fitzgerald owes much to our sense of what they might have been. Fitzgerald died at forty four, when none of his works could be found in a bookstore. A decade after his death all his books were all in print again and they still are. The attraction Frederick Rolfe exercises on so many is a little like that, but there is more. The more is his Catholicism, twisted, grotesque, almost unrecognizable at the end, but always the pulse beneath the skin of what he wrote.

Corvo made his mark in the *fin de siècle* literary circles of London, being associated with *The Yellow Book*, many of whose contributors began or ended as Catholics – Henry Harland, author of *The Cardinal's Snuff Box*, Oscar Wilde, Ambrose Beardsley, and Frederick Rolfe. *Stories Toto Told Me* are whimsical pieces replete with archaic spelling, Latinisms, and an effete outlook, which were much appreciated at the time. Rolfe published a sequel *In His Own Image* in 1900. Frederick Baron Corvo had not yet become the principal subject of his own fiction.

His most ambitious novels, *Hadrian VII* and *The Desire and Pursuit of the Whole*, are (in the case of the latter) a fictionalized account of his own life or (in the case of the former) a compensatory idealization, also known as wishful thinking. Always obsessively present in the foreground is the soul of the author. It is a sick soul.

Early in *Hadrian VII*, George Arthur Rose, Rolfe's *alter ego*, makes a general confession which, for all its self-accusation is an extended exercise in self-praise. The spurned acolyte is courted by bishops, apologized to by an obsequious cardinal, finally elected pope. Only governance of the whole Church and a choir of craven cardinals could imaginatively make up for Rolfe's clipped clerical career. Compared to the hero of *The Desire and Pursuit*, however, the Rolfe of *Hadrian VII* is in great spiritual and psychological shape.

The Desire and Pursuit was written in Venice. Rolfe had been taken there as a friend's guest, and he was destined never to leave the city alive. See Venice and die, indeed. He ran out of funds, he ran out of friends, he ran out of everything but an almost total self-absorption. The novel is an extended *j'accuse*, detailing the treachery and betrayal of which Rolfe, all innocent, has been the victim. To read it is to gain admission to at least an antechamber of hell.

Among the former benefactors pilloried in the Venetian novel – it is a tale of bitten hands – is Monsignor Robert Hugh Benson. Oddly, most who have written on the matter accept Rolfe's claim that Benson betrayed him. No one who reads Martindale's life of Benson could possibly think him guilty of anything more than excessive patience with a non-collaborating collaborator. They had agreed to do a life of Thomas à Becket together. Rolfe simply did not do anything on the project. Eventually, at the suggestion of the editor, Benson proposed dropping Rolfe's name from the title page but acknowledging his help. Only Frederick Rolfe could have been surprised that his failure to write the chapters he had agreed to write could have had any other result.

The ultimate puzzle about Frederick Rolfe, Baron Corvo, lies in the so-called "Venetian Letters." These are homosexual pornography in the form of letters to a British pervert in the hope of raising money. To such disfavor had this spoiled priest come. *Corruptio optimi pessima*? Not quite. From the beginning Rolfe's claim to a vocation seems to have sprung from a desire to dress up and star in liturgical spectacles.

Fiction arises from the oddest sources, but stories that feature the writer are not always of much interest to readers. Frederick Rolfe is far more studied than Robert Hugh Benson, a better writer, but this is largely due to the fascination of his almost diabolical personality. Rolfe's novels are read as documents about himself, not as imaginative inquiries into the meaning of human existence.

We are told that Rolfe received the last sacraments. God rest his soul. And keep *Hadrian VII* in print.

FRANCIS MARION CRAWFORD

*That an American Protestant born and raised in the shadow
of the Vatican should go to India to become a Catholic is surprising, but doubtless his early years had disposed Crawford
for conversion.*

THE last time I spoke to Russell Kirk I told him how delighted I
was to find his appreciation of Francis Marion Crawford in the
book John C. Moran devoted to that author. Kirk stressed
Crawford's status as a Romantic, and perhaps interest in the once
world-renowned author, now all but forgotten, can itself qualify
as romantic.

Crawford was born in Italy of American parents in 1854. His
father was a sculptor whose statue of Liberty adorns the Capitol
dome in Washington; recently it was brought down and refur-
bished with little effect on the reputations of either the father or
the son. Crawford was the nephew of Julia Ward Howe so that
when he was in this country he moved in most interesting circles.
Some of his schooling took place here, but it is difficult to think
of the author as an American, save in a Jamesian cosmopolitan
sense.

He spent a year at Cambridge, continued his studies in
Germany at Heidelberg, and in 1877, twenty-three years old,
returned to Rome. His father had died when Francis was three
years old and his mother soon married the American painter
Luther Terry; perhaps Francis fitted into the household only
imperfectly. He studied Sanskrit at the University of Rome –
Crawford was an extraordinary linguist, having some twenty
languages – and, in 1879, sailed for India. Early in his Indian
sojourn he converted to Roman Catholicism.

That an American Protestant born and raised in the shadow of the Vatican should go to India to become a Catholic is surprising, but doubtless his early years had disposed Crawford for conversion. After only a year in India, he returned to Rome, a young man without a clear plan of life. It was in 1881, while staying with the Howes in Boston that his literary career began almost whimsically. Asked to write down the stories of his Indian experience with which he had been entertaining his hosts, he produced his first novel, *Mr. Isaacs* (1882). It was the first of over forty books which would bring him fame, wealth, and vast cultural influence.

Crawford was thirty years old when he married Elizabeth Berdan, and the question arose as to where they should live. Eventually, the decision was made for Sorrento, where they settled into what was to be renamed Villa Crawford. Crawford was a remarkably fecund author who often wrote several novels a year. They enjoyed a remarkable popularity, enabling him to live in expatriate opulence on the Amalfi coast. Henry James was to visit him there and to feel an understandable resentment at Crawford's fame and affluence. It wasn't just that Crawford was prolific and James was not – each author produced a flood of fiction – but popular fame eluded James, though his critical reputation as the premier novelist of his day is now secure. Crawford on the other hand seems fated to survive in footnotes to James's published letters.

Crawford wrote against the mainstream insofar as this was defined by William Dean Howells. Howells, a remarkable writer, urged his fellow authors to concentrate on the social and moral upheaval in this country a century ago. Write American. Like James, Crawford set most of his stories abroad, but places and plights and atmosphere were utterly different in the two novelists. For Crawford, fiction presented another world, not a snapshot of this one, but his plots involved external action far more than inner moves of the Jamesian kind.

The so-called Saricinesca trilogy makes use of the Rome of Crawford's youth, a Rome which was still the capitol of the Papal

States, where old families combined in arranged marriages despite the promptings of romantic love, where duels were fought and mysterious characters operated under assumed identities, a Rome of art and architecture and opera. *Marzio's Crucifix* (1887) tells of a radical anti-clerical Socialist silversmith whose priest brother brings him a cardinal's commission for a silver crucifix. That such a man should spend his artistic life making religious articles becomes more than ironic when the silver crucifix becomes the means whereby Marzio is diverted from a nefarious plot.

Crawford did not use his novels to preach but the attitudes of many of his characters match his own. His views on the relation of art and religion, and on the likely effects of atheistic radicalism, are of more than passing interest. Crawford became a historian of modern Italy, writing extensively on the papacy and the effect of the Italian Republic on the Vatican. During his extensive lecture tour of the United States, his most popular talk dealt with Pope Leo XIII, the reigning pope.

A Crawford who could be at ease with his Yankee relatives managed as a novelist to write naturally from a Catholic perspective in a way that won him readers of all faiths and none. His biographer attributes Crawford's universal appeal to the muting of his religious beliefs. This seems unlikely, given his themes and the treatment of them. He lectured in Washington and in San Francisco, in New Orleans and Chicago, and dozens of points between (he spoke at Notre Dame in November of 1897).

Crawford died on Good Friday in 1909 at Sorrento and was buried there. He was a somewhat more robust Robert Louis Stevenson (who admired Crawford's writing); sickly throughout his life he was nevertheless incredibly active, always on the move whether on land or water.

His career provides an occasion to reflect on the nature of literary reputation. His posthumous popularity was brief, perhaps done a mortal blow by the moral upheaval of World War I. None of the novels that made him famous is in print today. His works have become collectibles. He is something of a cult figure for a few – the F. Marion Crawford Memorial Society was founded in 1975 – but by and large, in a way both his religion and his romantic outlook would have prepared him for, he has sunk into almost total oblivion.

Of course the same can be said of the vast majority of bestsellers of a quarter century ago, or of a decade ago. Novels are novelties that serve their purpose and then, for the most part, suffer the fate of periodicals. Nonetheless, you will find Crawford in any good library, certainly any Catholic university library, first editions marching along the shelves. Their titles may intrigue you. *Via Crucis. Zoroaster. Tale of a Lonely Parish. A Roman Singer. A Lady of Rome.* Certainly you will find *Saricinesca.* Maybe even *Casa Braccio.* Open it. A young nun flees the convent with her lover, employing a young woman's corpse to create the impression that she has died, not gone over the wall, and twenty years later the flown nun is dead and her husband and daughter Gloria live in Rome. The novel goes on to explore the intrigues and triangles and passions of Gloria and her circle. Eventually, she commits suicide and her father is left to contemplate how his sacrilegious deed of long ago has ruined many lives.

Villa Crawford, on the other hand, became a convent in which one of Crawford's daughters was a nun. He could have written a novel about that.

F. SCOTT FITZGERALD
The Authority of Failure

The Catholic formation came early, in St. Paul, but from the beginning it was at war with the hunger for upward mobility he acquired from both his parents.

"So we beat on, boats against the current, borne back ceaselessly into the past."

Thus ends one of the most perfect of American novels, *The Great Gatsby* by F. Scott Fitzgerald. The story is both a celebration of and a lament for a romantic view of life. Its sense of romance is thoroughly American: a dream of wealth and social grace and expensive diversion in exotic places. Fitzgerald presents powerfully and from the inside this national longing to be elsewhere, otherwise, higher, engaged in some enhanced mode of existence. At the same time, he chronicles the necessary defeat of such dreams. The first aspect he owed to his country, the second to his faith.

F. Scott Fitzgerald ended as a lapsed Catholic but not before his imagination had been formed by the faith. The Catholic formation came early, in St. Paul, but from the beginning it was at war with the hunger for upward mobility he acquired from both his parents.

He grew up in a series of homes on and around Summit Avenue. In the longish story, "Winter Dreams," his hero Dexter White might be Fitzgerald, the caddy fallen in love with the member's daughter. The phrase "shabbily genteel" comes to mind when one thinks of his family. But they sacrificed for Scott. His prep school, Newman, no longer exists, but he went on to Princeton.

The early lives of Fitzgerald would lead you to believe that he left his religion behind him when he went off to college. The excellent biography of Matthew Bruccoli corrects this, but then we should have noticed the influence of Shane Leslie and the dedication of the first novel, *This Side of Paradise*, to Monsignor Sigourney Fay. The novel itself is shot through with a sense of the stakes of life. The devil makes a personal appearance. Bruccoli tells us that Fitzgerald had signed on with Fay for a wartime mission to Moscow on behalf of the Vatican that never came off.

The practice of Catholicism seems to have just seeped away. He and Zelda Sayre, the Southern belle he had desperately pursued and, unluckily, won, were married in the sacristy of St. Patrick's cathedral. She accepted him when the novel he had gone back to St. Paul to finish was accepted for publication. During this time, he often visited a priest on the faculty of the major seminary at the end of Summit Avenue. Could he have lived with his family and not practiced his faith? In a letter to Edmund Wilson he says he no longer tells his crystalline beads, but this may tell us more about Wilson than about Fitzgerald.

Success came immediately and overwhelmingly, transforming the beautiful young Fitzgeralds into celebrities. Back east on Long Island the party raged on. The second novel had an ominous motto: The victor belongs to the spoils. In the depths of dissipation, Fitzgerald achieved the imaginative and moral distance that enabled him to write *Gatsby*. In it the east becomes a metaphor for dissolution; the remedy is the one taken by Nick Carraway at the end, a return to the moral geography of the Midwest. Writing of the return trip home from college at Christmas, Fitzgerald wrote of leaving Chicago on the last leg of the long journey when the train headed northwest through the snow to innocence.

From the pinnacle of early success, his life spiraled down. Zelda went mad, Scott went to Hollywood. In the early '30s, when his star had fallen, he published a series of essays that became *The Crack Up*. Nowhere is the Catholic imagination of Fitzgerald more evident than in these cool reflections on where his life went wrong. Cool but bewildered. He sees himself as the man who did not make the team in college, as the soldier who never got overseas, as the parvenu who might frolic with the *nouveaux riches* but was forever conscious that "the rich are different from you and me." Writing during the Depression, he toyed with economic reasons for his fate. But throbbing beneath the self-examination is a persistent religious sensibility. Who but a Catholic could speak of his ordeal as the dark night of the soul (his mention of it propelled the phrase into the secular vocabulary)? Who but a Catholic, thinking of the noonday devil, would quote Psalm 90 in the Latin Vulgate? The story "Babylon Revisited" evokes a wispier Dante regarding the scene where the moral battle was lost.

Tender Is the Night, the story of what went wrong with him and Zelda, appeared in 1934 when superficially grimmer fare was wanted. When he died in 1940, at forty four, he was a burnt-out case, not even successful (as Faulkner had been) in Hollywood. The Pat Hobby stories, a wry self-portrait, are wildly comic yet melancholy too. His books were out of print, he was forgotten, he was at work on *The Last Tycoon*.

When Dorothy Parker came to the wake she looked down at the waxen face and said, "The poor sonofabitch." She was of course quoting from *Gatsby*, with all the dread of one lapsed Catholic at the death of another.

Fitzgerald put Hemingway (himself briefly a Catholic) on to his publisher, Charles Scribner. Ever after, an imagined version of the Oak Park novelist he so admired functioned as a kind of artistic conscience for Fitzgerald. Ernest, he once said, speaks with the authority of success. I speak with the authority of failure. But is any recognized failure ever complete?

Reading of Fitzgerald's last days, I find myself hoping that he will find himself, go back to St. Paul, rediscover the roots of his imagination, recover his faith. Of course it is not a question of geography. Still, it is a comfort to know that his remains, at first refused burial in a Catholic cemetery, were eventually transferred to consecrated ground. Cardinal Baum, who authorized it, sought in Fitzgerald's writing the hope that he had not entirely left the faith of his fathers. He lies now in a Maryland churchyard, with Zelda beside him and now their daughter too. "So we beat on, boats against the current . . ." Let's hope that they were all safe in harbor at the end.

September 1996 marked the centenary of the birth of F. Scott Fitzgerald. The thought of the writer who became all but identified with flaming youth and the roaring Twenties as a hundred years old rattles the imagination. When he died, Fitzgerald seemed to have outlived his material and to have been reduced to the role of hack writer on the fringes of the Hollywood establishment. Not even his friends would have imagined that he would emerge as the most important American writer of his generation.

Of course it would be Hemingwayesque to rank the writers of the twenties and thirties as if they were contenders for the heavyweight championship. One need not disparage Faulkner and Hemingway and dos Passos and Cather in order to notice that Fitzgerald seems to have transcended the limitations of his times more surely than they. Whether more biographies and studies have been written about Hemingway or Fitzgerald is a nice question, and it is fitting that there is a joint newsletter devoted to the two of them.

Hemingway became a Catholic when he married for the second time, but it does not seem to have taken in any profound sense. Imaginatively he had already appropriated the faith in *The Sun Also Rises*, set during the festival of San Firmin in Pamplona and the most religious and Catholic of his novels. Fitzgerald became what the Australians call a retired Catholic. He and Zelda Sayre married in the sacristy of St. Patrick's, and their daughter was baptized in St. Paul, but there is not much evidence of anything like an ordinary Catholic life on his part. But all three now lie in consecrated ground in Maryland and their fate, like ours, is in the hands of God.

I have sometimes thought that Fitzgerald was a "Kennedy Catholic" before the time. Although he went to a now-defunct Catholic prep school it was the Princeton from which he never graduated that conferred on him his surface scale of values. The influence of Edmund Wilson, ever jealous, often malignant, prompted Fitzgerald to mock his own origins. Under the influence of Shane Leslie and the priest to whom he dedicated his first novel there was an effort to acquire a Catholic sensibility. But Princeton prevailed. Yet somehow he was Catholic to the soles of his feet, and it comes out again and again in the writing.

The most striking thing about Fitzgerald, as a moralist, was his ability to gain imaginative distance from the forces that drove his own life. He had a mad American appetite for money and fun and social ascendancy, and all of these are coldly analyzed and condemned in his work. "The victor belongs to the spoils," in the mordant motto of *The Beautiful and the Damned*. His very style exhibits this duality, combining often in the same sentence lyricism and matter-of-factness. Pervading it all was the continuing hunger for that which the singular objects of appetite cannot give. He associates this with the past of the country and doubtless with his own past too. "So we beat on, boats against the current, borne back ceaselessly into the past."

I have often wondered why, when his life smashed and his wife went mad and his drinking got out of control, he did not go back to Minnesota and get reoriented. It is not because, as his great contemporary said, you can't go home again. Very likely we can't go anywhere else, finally. But there is a Minnesota of the mind and that accompanied Fitzgerald to his premature death in the apartment of his mistress just before Christmas in 1940.

The debt that lovers of American literature owe Matthew Bruccoli is enormous, and this is especially true because of his long devotion to Fitzgerald. A definitive edition of the works is appearing from Cambridge University Press, thanks to Bruccoli.

And it is thanks to him that we have the best biography, a facsimile edition of the ledger, and all the previously uncollected stories. We must marvel at the sheer industry and output of this allegedly flighty author.

Too many have accepted Fitzgerald's own low estimate of most of his short fiction. I think this is unfortunate. After all, he was appraising it by his own high standards. I have recently reread the Pat Hobby stories, written for Esquire for a fraction of his usual fee. Hobby is a failed screenwriter, a con man in the kingdom of con (I will resist saying Condom), improvident, mistrusted, triumphant in his failures. Did Fitzgerald fear that this is what he himself might become? The mastery exhibited in these slight, extremely funny, stories was the best exorcism of that fear.

At his death he was engaged in writing what we must now call *The Love of the Last Tycoon, A Western*. This unfinished book, like *Tender Is the Night*, falls short of his masterpiece, *The Great Gatsby*, but it is infinitely preferable to shelves of finished novels. And Bruccoli presents us, as he did in his first book on the composition of *Tender Is the Night*, the author at work, constructing his story, revising his text, pondering its implications.

Scott Fitzgerald one hundred years old! It boggles the mind. May his literary reputation know many centuries more. And as for him, may he rest in peace.

FORD MADOX FORD

*The view Ford attributes to Conrad was surely his own –
"every work of art has – must have – a profound moral
purpose."*

"This is the saddest story I have ever heard." With this haunting
sentence Ford Madox Ford began what he always considered his
best novel, *The Good Soldier*. One of his biographers considered
Ford's the saddest story, and used the phrase as the title of his life
of the writer.

He lived from 1873 to 1939, published over eighty books,
knew everyone. His grandfather was a painter, his father a musi-
cologist, he was related by marriage to the Rossettis, Dante and
Christina, he was raised in the atmosphere of Victorian and pre-
Raphaelite art, he published his first book at the age of eighteen.

Ford collaborated with Joseph Conrad on several novels when
the Polish-born author was unsure of his command of English.
But, as the memoir Ford wrote in the year of Conrad's death
makes clear, it was the technique of fiction that fascinated the
two men. A story should read the way it would sound if told by a
good storyteller – that was their shared theory. Later Conrad novels have as their distinctive trait the narrative voice of one who,
over a bottle, is recalling the events of the story.

This technique called for a progression quite different from
the chronological. When you tell your spouse about your day, you
constantly interrupt yourself, recall something that happened
earlier than what you were telling, move back and forth, yet
somehow drive forward to the point. *The Good Soldier* puts this
technique to masterful use.

The best art conceals itself, as Horace knew, and the same can be said of artlessness in fiction. Ford's narrator recalls events that have somewhat the effect of Agatha Christie's *Who Killed Roger Ackroyd?* at the end of which the narrator is surprisingly revealed to be the murderer. Ford's narrator tells of the way in which he was betrayed, by a friend, by his wife, and Ford manages to invest his narrator at the start of the telling with the same naivetÉ he had at the start of the events narrated. The motto of the novel is taken from the Beatitudes: *Beati Immaculati* – blessed are the pure of heart.

If the novel is a *tour de force*, it is only retrospectively that we think so. In the reading we are swept into the account and are not conscious of how the effects are achieved. The view Ford attributes to Conrad was surely his own – "every work of art has – must have – a profound moral purpose." And, describing the sense of achievement Conrad must have felt at the end, all the reverses temporary, the achievements as lasting as mortal man is capable of, Ford concludes, "That is to be granted what we Papists call the cross of the happy death."

The false note here – "cross" for "grace" – is indicative of Ford's unsureness about the religion to which he was converted at the age of eighteen. As his latest biographer Alan Judd puts it, "He was received into the Roman Catholic Church later that same year in Paris and remained nominally a Catholic for the rest of his life, though his practice was irregular and his belief at best ambiguous." When his daughter Christina went to school to the nuns, he was nervous, and indeed she became a nun and remained one all her long life.

Ford himself left his first wife, lived notoriously with Stella Bowen and spent the last decade of his life with Janice Biala. He was, in the phrase, susceptible to women, and vice versa. His last mistress, an "unreconstructed Jew," may not be the best source of what Ford's faith consisted of, yet she gives strong testimony of it almost inadvertently. He was not practicing, she wrote, but he preferred Catholicism because it was clear enough so that you could break away from it and know you had. He admired the Church's organization, and he had a devotion to Mary. She concludes by saying that Ford believed in Catholicism philosophically.

One might better say, imaginatively. Ford saw in fidelity the main inspiration of Conrad's fiction, fidelity and its opposite. Betrayal and treachery, a person's failure to be or do what he morally must – these are what excited Ford's imagination. And in *The Good Soldier* he magnificently developed it through the eyes of one betrayed.

Ford was sixty-six when he died, and that is surprising, since he seemed to have lived three or four lives and to have known everyone. In *Portraits from Life,* he writes of Henry James, Stephen Crane, W. H. Hudson, Joseph Conrad, Thomas Hardy, H. G. Wells, John Galsworthy, D. H. Lawrence, Turgenev, Dreiser, and Swinburne. He went off to World War I at nearly forty years of age and in the post-War World, in Paris, edited the *transatlantic review* and knew Joyce and Hemingway and Pound. In *A Moveable Feast*, Hemingway repays Ford's kindness in the coin of resentment, but then only the author comes out of that book unscathed.

Parade's End, Ford's tetralogy of World War I, is autobiographical in part. In it he puts before us the enormous social and moral upheaval that the war was. These four novels have recently been issued in a convenient single volume by Everyman's Library. They are to English involvement in the first world war, what Powell's *A Dance to the Music of Time* and Waugh's *Sword of Honour* are to the second. (Why would it seem so odd to add *The Winds of War* and *War and Remembrance* to that little list?)

Ford also wrote a trilogy about Henry VIII, which bears the collective title *The Fifth Queen*. Here is Ford on the events that produced the great separation of the English church from Rome. That theological differences should be embedded in the lust and pride of men and women does not seem anomalous to him.

Greene compared the aged Ford to an impossibly old veteran of the Napoleonic wars who could tell us of long ago mythical times from his own experience. Ford wrote a great many reminiscences, aiming not at impersonal factual truth, but at conveying what people and events had meant to him. They have the truth of his impressions.

In this country he was close to Alan Tate and Caroline Gordon and the young Robert Lowell, Catholics all, at the time, but it was Mount Olivet College in Michigan that had the sense to snare this literary treasure and give him a classroom as well as an honorary degree.

When his life ended, he could not have felt the serenity he attributed to Conrad at the end of his. He does not, alas, seem to have been granted the cross of a happy death. Ford asked for no priest and received no last rites.

God of course moves in mysterious ways, even more mysteriously than the narrative line in a Ford novel. It is pleasant to think of him there in Deauville, in the Clinique St François, cared for by nuns. And there was his daughter Christina too, in her convent, doubtless praying for the talented, generous, weak, loyal, wavering, great-hearted man who was her father. His may not have been the saddest story, but like his fiction it had, however fitfully, a strong moral purpose.

ETIENNE GILSON

The purpose of the Institute, he said, is to produce people who can read the Divine Comedy intelligently. That sounds like a mot, but it is a veritable summa of wisdom.

IN the Collège de France there is a lecture room whose seats descend in rows to a desk on which a podium is flanked by two green-shaded lamps. There at the beginning of this century Henri Bergson lectured in the evening to the elite of Paris. This room was chosen as the site of a posthumous tribute to Etienne Gilson, Catholic philosopher, medieval historian, member of the French Academy. Participants were to make remarks of no more than ten minutes duration. I myself spoke on Gilson as an English stylist. I was followed by a man with a gleam in his eye. There is no more terrible sight than an intellectual gripping the podium with a large manuscript before him, his body English a protest against any time limitation on his remarks. This fellow droned on and on as hostility grew and finally shouts of anger and annoyance were heard. To no effect. In a similar situation, Gilson had a band strike up the Marseillaise, thus ending the proceedings.

It was fitting that the scholarly class should have been represented in its comic and slightly mad form on this occasion, if only as contrast to the way in which Etienne Gilson (1884–1978) combined vast scholarship with an earthy bonhomie and punctilious erudition with self-effacement. He was one of the most learned men of his times but he never lost the common touch. No one would have had to remind him of the brevity of mortal man's attention span.

Gilson was a quintessential Frenchman whose research almost predictably began with Descartes. The Father of Modern Philosophy prided himself with having put away the Scholastic training he had received from the Jesuits at La Flèche, wiped the slate of his mind clean and started from ground zero. Gilson noticed that this was far from being the case. Indeed, he found Descartes to be all but unintelligible apart from the Scholasticism he professed to have abandoned. Thus began Gilson's scholarly interest in the Middle Ages.

It is difficult to imagine what medieval studies and our understanding of the thought of the Schoolmen would have been if Gilson had not brought his enormous energy, talent, and verve to the Middle Ages.

His first contribution to the field was to refute the notion that Scholasticism was a monolith to which a series of thinkers subscribed. Taken one at a time, medieval authors revealed their diversity. There were, Gilson argued, medieval philosophies, in the plural – he wrote books on many of the great figures. He demonstrated by his work that the Middle Ages can be ignored by the historian only at his peril.

It had become received opinion that for about a thousand years of human history not much happened by way of philosophy. This strange myth still has many in its grip – as Regine Pernoud constantly reminds us – but after Gilson ignorance of medieval philosophy is culpable. In responding to this received opinion, Gilson drew attention to the unstated presuppositions of contemporary philosophy which set the face of modern thinkers against their medieval counterparts.

One of the assumptions of much modern thought is that the serious use of the mind must lead to the abandonment of religious faith. In most cases, this is an unexamined prejudice. Well, the thinkers of the Middle Ages assumed that the serious use of the mind would lend support to the faith. Moreover, revealed truth provided intimations of philosophical truths undreamt of by pagans. Gilson became a champion of what he called Christian

Philosophy – the thinking that goes on within the ambience of the faith and is supported by, indeed inspired, by it. His Gifford Lectures, *The Spirit of Medieval Philosophy* are an eloquent statement of this position.

Gilson's academic career began at Lille but after World War I, during which he was taken prisoner, he moved to the Sorbonne. Early on he wrote a summary work of the thought of St. Thomas Aquinas, *Le thomisme* (*The Christian Philosophy of St. Thomas Aquinas*), a work whose subsequent editions would provide the trajectory of Gilson's own philosophical development. Gilson first visited America in 1926 and was welcomed and feted at Harvard and Virginia. But it was the founding of the Pontifical Institute of Mediaeval Studies at Toronto in 1929 that was to make Gilson's impact on North America wide and deep. From then on, his academic year would be divided between France and Canada. The Institute gave him the opportunity, thanks to the Basilian Fathers, to turn his own scholarly practices into a program.

The purpose of the Institute, he said, is to produce people who can read the Divine Comedy intelligently. That sounds like a *mot*, but it is a veritable summa of wisdom. The work of Dante is the fruit of the 13th century, and all those that had gone before, and fully to appreciate it requires an understanding of its antecedents.

It is the mark of the truly original scholar that he comes to lament the company he is forced to keep. The pursuit of truth, painstaking research, the years of patient reading, are meant to open the mind to wisdom and to enable the wise man to communicate with the simple. The dark side of academe is that it is a guild whose skills and techniques can be taught to almost anyone with minimal talent and their ultimate point easily lost sight of. Hence the contrast between the pedant determined to speak for half an hour in tribute of a man who would have guffawed at the spectacle. Gilson was a wise man whose late works are aimed generally at the intelligent, not the learned.

Gilson came to have negative thoughts about the Thomistic tradition as well as about many of his contemporary Thomists.

In an exchange of letters with Henri DeLubac, edited after Gilson's death by the cardinal, Gilson is prompted to side with DeLubac against those, like Pius XII, who had misgivings about the Jesuit's doctrine of the supernatural.

Similarly, in the posthumously published correspondence with Jacques Maritain, the editor includes a letter Gilson wrote to Father Armand Maurer in which he says that only after half a century did he understand the difference between Maritain and himself. Gilson saw himself as "ascertaining the authentic meaning of St. Thomas's doctrine, which only history can do; during all that time, he [Maritain] was considering himself a true disciple of St. Thomas because he was *continuing* his thought."

This is a contrast, not a conflict, and can serve as an epitaph to the two great French students of Thomas Aquinas, Jacques Maritain and Etienne Gilson.

GRAHAM GREENE

Like many writers, Greene resisted the appellation of Catholic novelist, since he did not want readers to be seeking catechetical exactitude in his stories.

In what is arguably his first Catholic novel, *The Power and the Glory*, Graham Greene contrasts a weak, alcoholic fugitive priest with his austere pursuer. There are other contrasts in the book as well – between the hunted man who cannot escape the demands of his ministry and his soft, comfortable self before the revolution; between the second nocturne tale of martyrdom read by pious children and the real-life flawed candidate for the firing squad with whiskey on his breath – but the basic contrast is between the political and the religious. All efforts to see the significance of human life in this-world terms are inadequate to the way it really is.

Other Catholic novels are *The Heart of the Matter, The End of the Affair*, and *A Burnt-Out Case*. The series comes to an end in 1973 with *The Honorary Consul*. Greene still had years to live and many books to write, but his imagination had switched from a religious into a political gear.

The *Heart of the Matter* takes its motto from Charles Peguy. "At the very heart of Christianity is the sinner. No one is more competent on the matter of Christianity than the sinner – unless it be the saint." Major Scobie damns himself out of pity for a waif-like war widow in colonial Africa. Greene is at his best presenting Catholicism through the medium of failed Catholics, sinners. Faith is not meant to produce sinners, of course, but being a sinner is a condition of entry.

Like many writers, Greene resisted the appellation of Catholic novelist, since he did not want readers to be seeking catechetical exactitude in his stories. To be a spokesman for the faith is a very different thing from having an imagination permeated with belief.

The persistent theme of Greene's fiction is betrayal, and sin is the ultimate treachery. Disloyalty to friends and country provide variations on the theme, and they are all Greene has left when he reverses the outlook of *The Power and the Glory*. The motto of *The Honorary Consul* is taken from Thomas Hardy. "All things merge in one another – good into evil, generosity into justice, religion into politics . . ."

Religion into politics. That merger deprives Greene's later fiction of the pulse of the novels that begin with the story of the Mexican martyr. During the war, Greene was a spy, and afterward he defended the homosexual traitors Burgess and Maclean. There began then his odd flirtation with totalitarian governments and Central American dictators and his increasingly virulent anti-Americanism. This seems to have had its origin in the pique he felt at being kept out of the United States because of his brief Oxford affiliation with the Communist Party.

Not entirely, of course. In *The Lawless Roads*, the non-fiction account of his trip to revolutionary Mexico, Greene sees America as the great Pelagian colossus to the north, where sin is unrecognized and the purpose of life is earthbound, materialist, glitzy. Mexico, backward, savage, and bloody, is a place where the drama of salvation can be played out.

In *The Third Man*, the put-down of America is just British snobbery – Americans like ice cream – as later in the prologue to *The Comedians* it will be conveyed through a comic also-ran presidential candidate. In *The Quiet American*, the Vietnam novel, the eponymous American causes havoc by trying to do good, but there is no theological contrast to this chuckle-headed Pelagianism, just a lofty and unearned superiority on the part of the Brit narrator, with his opium habit and native mistress.

Graham Greene became a Catholic prior to his marriage. He was a journalist in Nottingham at the time, and his account of the *terminus ad quem* of this conversion can be found in the first of his uninformative autobiographical volumes, *A Sort of Life*. The priest to whom he went had the improbable name of Trollope (perhaps this is a little joke). Greene found the cathedral gloomy and the priest repellant, fat, soft, smooth skinned. He turns out to be a converted actor and Greene warms to him. "It was quite a while before I realized that my first impression was totally false and that I was facing the challenge of an inexplicable goodness."

Greene describes the instructions he took as a time of battle. He didn't disbelieve in Christ; he didn't even believe there was a God. What happened? "I can only remember that in January 1926 I became convinced of the probable existence of something we call God, though now I dislike the word with all its anthropo-morphic associations and prefer Chardin's 'Noosphere' . . ." Greene is writing more than forty years later, of course, and he says his memory fails him. Among the "anthropomorphic associ-ations" he dislikes would appear to be the Incarnation. If this were an accurate description, it sounds like a timid Deism rather than a conversion to Roman Catholicism.

One learns to distrust Greene's accounts of his own life, par-ticularly the most personal aspects of it. He manages to remember his wife's name in his memoirs, but his children are anonymous if alluded to at all. He left his wife and took up with a woman he delighted in calling his mistress. *The Burnt-Out Case* tells of a famous architect who goes to Africa to escape his repu-tation as a Catholic artist. He no longer believes what supposedly inspires him and he seeks desperately in a leper colony for what he has lost. Is that Greene? Perhaps.

Just as Greene's anti-Americanism led him to express a prefer-ential option for the reds (*The Human Factor*), so in matters religious he flirted with the heterodox and the bizarre (Chardin).

It is depressing to think that his radical chic and trendy anti-Americanism, the distancing of himself from his all too famous

Catholicism, was a bid for the Nobel Prize he never won and surely deserved more than most who received it.

Greene was technically one of the greatest writers of our time. When I was learning to write, I analyzed his novels, breaking them into their components, studying the way he achieved his effects. To this day I have to check myself from writing poor imitations of his prose. I cannot think of a better technical model for an aspiring writer.

I have not mentioned the plays, or the film scripts, the essays, the occasional writings. Greene was a gentleman enamored of the moral slums, but he ended what he had not wanted to be, a consummate man of letters. And a Catholic writer – of a sort.

PAUL HORGAN

*Writers could perhaps be divided into those who sentimen-
talize childhood and those who see it as the frightening time
when we become aware of our own and others' capacity for
evil. A child drowns a kitten, encounters a flasher, sees the
cruelty done to a retarded friend, has a delightful uncle who
commits suicide.*

When Paul Horgan was given the Laetare Medal by the
University of Notre Dame in 1976, it may have been the first
public recognition of this Catholic writer by his Church. Horgan
was born in 1903 and had been publishing poetry and fiction for
forty years. In his adopted New Mexico – the family moved there
for his father's health in 1915 – he was honored and feted; he had
been invited to lecture at the Iowa Writer's School, and from 1960
was involved in Wesleyan University's Center for Advanced
Studies. Why did Catholics wait until he was seventy three to recognize this writer?

The immediate occasion was the magnificent biography Paul
Horgan had published in 1975, *Lamy of Santa Fe.* The book won
him a Pulitzer Prize as well as the Laetare Medal. It told the story
of the man who had inspired Willa Cather's *Death Comes for the
Archbishop*, a French missionary who, after beginning his apostolic
work in Ohio, became the first bishop of Santa Fe, a diocese that
covered a good part of the eventual western United States.

In extenuation of Horgan's apparent neglect by his co-
religionists, it must be said that if he was not precisely a late
bloomer as an artist, there was for some time indecision as to
which art he would pursue. In 1923, Horgan returned to his
native New York and entered the Eastman School of Music in

Rochester, where he studied for three years. This musical background was important throughout his life. *Encounters with Stravinsky* appeared in 1972, but he had met the musician in 1958.

But music was not to be Paul Horgan's primary art. Perhaps he would be a painter. Throughout his life he produced watercolors, and a friend from boyhood was the painter Peter Hurd, whose portrait in words he published in 1965. He published poetry and then turned to the novel. *The Fault of Angels* won the Harper Prize Novel Contest in 1933, and for the next ten years, until his wartime service caused him to lay aside his imaginative writing, he published ten books.

World War II had a decisive effect on Horgan's career as a writer. He did not publish a work of fiction for ten long years, and it was his history of the Rio Grande, *Great River*, published in 1954, that earned him his first Pulitzer.

His next popular success was the historical novel, *A Distant Trumpet*, which in many ways is more history than novel. This involvement in history was to continue in a series of narratives of the South West, culminating in the magnificent *Lamy of Santa Fe*.

Horgan's wartime career in Washington widened his circle of friends; his musical and operatic beginnings gave him entree to the world of musical production. It was in his capacity as Director of Wesleyan's Center for Advanced Study that he was in Rome and found himself in St. Peter's at the opening of a session of Vatican II in 1963. An account of this is to be found in his essay, "*Roma Barocca.*" His judgment of the music was mordant.

> The several choirs were involved by turns, all equally strident, faithless to pitch, indifferent to rhythm, tempo, and ensemble. Female voices were heard, sounding like matronly crows answering the quavering gobbles of their male kind. But like redemption, a white blade of pure

tone from a boy cut through to the vault. The Sistine
Choir had once been incomparable, according to
eighteenth-century travellers who wrote to say so. The
child Mozart went ravening away to write down what he
had heard.

A disenchanted Catholic? Not at all, just a man cursed with a
sensitive ear. But it is his eye of which we are principally aware.
"Before us in the shower of light falling from within the lappets
of the baldochino, the shift and weave, the unfolding of the
Pontifical High Mass was beginning as Paul VI, attended by
prelates who managed the folds of his huge white and gold cope,
censed the altar at all its dimensions; for it stood there as an
image of the body of Christ upon which the holy sacrifice itself
would once again be enacted." He was also making sketches for
future watercolors during the Pope's two-hour-long address to the
Council fathers.

One introducing himself to Paul Horgan might do worse than
begin with the essays collected in 1993, under the title *Tracings*.
Lamy of Santa Fe is a must, of course, summing up as it does the
study and wisdom of an already long life and bringing them to
bear on an extraordinary churchman who provides a lens through
which we can see Horgan's beloved Southwest. It is interesting to
learn that the young Horgan met the much older Willa Cather in
New Mexico.

His studies of Peter Hurd and of Igor Stravinsky give a sense
of Horgan's cultural range. *A Distant Trumpet* could serve as tran-
sition into Horgan's non-historical fiction.

What is to be said of the novels? Consider two trilogies, the so-
called Richard novels and then those brought together under the
collective title of *Mountain Standard Time*. The novels in the latter
date from the first, pre-war period. They share the common
Horgan theme: evil, sin, original and actual. Few writers can put so
relentlessly and simply before their reader human evil, that of the
individual, that of the crowd. The novels turn on a woman's seduc-

tion by a traveling salesman, social agitation in the Depression, and then in *The Common Heart*, the story of a family like Horgan's own, coming from the east into Mountain Standard Time.

The Richard novels, written over a twenty-five year span, add up to a single *bildungsroman*, a growing up: childhood, boyhood, young manhood. Writers could perhaps be divided into those who sentimentalize childhood and those who see it as the frightening time when we become aware of our own and others' capacity for evil. A child drowns a kitten, encounters a flasher, sees the cruelty done to a retarded friend, has a delightful uncle who commits suicide . . .

Horgan's is a powerful moral imagination, and his characters disturb by their simple verisimilitude and what they tell us about ourselves. But it would be wrong to convey the notion that Horgan's is a world of black pessimism. It is human weakness, our capacity for evil, that makes goodness stand out in all its wonder. He rejected the notion that *Far from Cibola* was a "Proletarian novel." "The book has nothing to do with masses, or classes, or crippling concepts of man as a being without a soul. It is a poem with as many subjects as it has characters; but the subject underlying all others, though never stated, is human charity – 'the greatest of these.'"

The third chapter of *Things as They Are* bears the title "Muzza," which is the way the retarded boy John addresses his mother. Richard is John's friend and hears the other boys chant, "John, John, the dog-faced one," and it is that taunt that makes him realize that John is different. But this does not affect his own attitude toward the boy next door even though he is vaguely aware that John's mother is bribing him to be her son's friend. On the first day of school, Mrs. Burley asks Richard to accompany John to school.

That first day is a disaster. It becomes unmistakable that John is incapable of doing what other kids his age do. Richard takes John home after school, and on the way they stop at a candy store. When they emerge, they are confronted by other boys who begin to tease John. Richard and John run off, but they are pursued and cornered in a garage, where the boys turn a hose on John. He is knocked down.

> "Get up, dogface," yelled one of the boys.
>
> Obediently John got up, keeping his eyes closed, suffering all that must come to him. The hose column toppled him over again. Striking his face, blows of water knocked his head about until it seemed to fly apart.

The boys strip John, tearing off his clothes, and then turn the hose on him again, making him spin and slide on the oily floor of the garage. Richard runs for help, bringing back Mrs. Burley, and she gathers her son, dripping and blue with cold, into her arms. "Muzza," he said thickly. "Oh, Muzza, Muzza."

John is wrapped up and taken home and put to bed. He develops a fever. Mrs. Burley is grateful to Richard, but the boy senses that she has begun to accept the tormentors' view of her son.

Thus far we have been given a vivid, heart-wrenching scene, and many authors would be content to leave it there. An unfortunate child, cruel bullies, a steadfast friend. But we are reading Paul Horgan, and the situation and its potential for evil are far from exhausted.

John's fever worsens, and he dies. There is a private burial. Richard is asked to select some of John's toys for himself. Mrs. Burley talks to him about her dead son, expressing the thought that it was best that he die.

> "Garsh, when you see cripples trying to get along, and the sick people who never get well, you wonder why they can't be spared, and just die."
>
> The appalling truth was gathering in me. I stared at her while she continued.
>
> "John was always frail, and when those horrid boys turned on him and he caught that chill, and it went into

pneumonia, his father and I did everything to save him, but it was not enough. We had to see him go."

Clutching John's beautiful power boat in both arms, I cowered a little away from her and said, "You never sent for a doctor, though."

A sharp silence cuts its way between us. She put one hand on her breast and held herself. At last she said in a dry, bitter voice, "Is that what is being said?"

"Doctor Grauer always comes when I am sick."

She put her hand to her mouth. Her eyes were afire like those of a trapped cat.

"Richard?" she whispered against her fingers, "what are you thinking? Don't you believe we loved John?"

I said, inevitably, "Did you have him die?"

The poor woman reacts violently, striking out at the accusing boy, who dances away, dropping and breaking the toy. Then he escapes from the house and runs home, "frightened by what I had exposed."

This novel was published in 1952 and reprinted with the other novels in the Richard Trilogy in 1990. Richard's viewpoint, the moral universe in which Paul Horgan's story moves, is quite simply that which characterized our civilization for centuries. It is significant that, even after the Holocaust and other mass-scale slaughters of our time, Horgan is able to create circumstances that we ourselves might occupy and where a deed is done that appeals to the same rationale as Auschwitz and the Hemlock Society.

JAMES JOYCE

When his faith went, he made a religion of his writing and ruthlessly sacrificed all else to it. Through years of exile, poverty, and difficulties getting published, he persisted, and eventually recognition and fame came.

THE movie made of "The Dead," the longest story in James Joyce's collection *Dubliners*, had a nostalgic attraction that might have surprised its author. His short stories do not so much tell a story in a traditional, i.e. De Maupassant, manner, as they put before us events in such a way that an "epiphany" occurs, and the characters are revealed as banal, trapped, thwarted. Gabriel Conway, in "The Dead," is Joyce's portrait of himself as he would have become if he had remained in Ireland.

Joyce (1882–1941) was one of the greatest writers of the 20th century, whether greatness be gauged by influence or achievement. He was an occasional poet, a one-time dramatist, content with a single collection of stories, and the author of three novels that move from autobiography, through myth, to a self-contained linguistic universe.

James Joyce was obsessed with Ireland and the Roman Catholic Church, both of which he left, but neither of which would let him go – at least as an artist. The apostate and exile could only write by brooding about his native land and the faith he had abandoned at the age of sixteen.

Hugh Kenner, in a magnificent book entitled *The Pound Era*, a loving and sympathetic account of literary modernism, perhaps gives Ezra Pound more credit than he deserves for the movement's success. Were one to pick a patron of its poetry it would be T. S. Eliot and the uncontested master of modern prose fiction is James Joyce. (Kenner wrote books on both, as it happens, and I am not suggesting he would think otherwise.)

The Portrait of the Artist as a Young Man tells the story of Stephen Dedalus from infancy to the attainment of his university degree. An earlier version of the novel was called *Stephen Hero*. It is autobiographical and may be read as Joyce's imaginative reconstruction of himself. So obsessed is the book with Stephen that we never learn the names of his many brothers and sisters, although his parents, particularly his father, are vividly portrayed, both unflatteringly. Stephen cannot believe that he is the true son of such parents.

Through long years of Jesuit education, Stephen moves from "college" (Joyce entered Conglowes College at the age of six and a half) through the university when Stephen is poised to take flight from Ireland, from family, from faith, "to forge in the smithy of my soul the uncreated conscience of my race."

Whatever intellectual difficulties Stephen has with the faith are consequent on a plunge into carnality which, at sixteen, seems phenomenally precocious. Solitary sins, the frequenting of prostitutes, an obsession with sex that clouds his mind and heart, are brought to the magnificently presented retreat featuring the Four Last Things – heaven, hell, death, and judgment. The sermon on hell in the *Portrait* will touch the heart of the most hardened sinner – and it touches Stephen, bringing him back to the sacraments by way of a confession characterized by a considerate and compassionate Capuchin.

If one were to compare this confession scene with the hundreds of others written by flown Catholics, for example, that in Fitzgerald's story "Absolution," he would be struck by Joyce's artistic integrity. His Jesuit preacher is given pages of the book, and there is not a false note in his sermons. Stephen, having repented, throws himself into an orgy of religious practices which he cannot sustain, and then it is back to the fleshpots. Only then are dogmatic doubts entertained.

In recent years, there has been a flood of fiction by discontented or lapsed Catholics, a dominant note of which is to blame the Church for her teaching on sexual morality. Since this is the morality of the Old as well as the New Testament, the complaint often seems uninformed. But sex is at the center of the discontent. The suggestion seems to be that once a person is free from all those "shalt nots," from the humiliation of acknowledging one's sins and asking God's forgiveness in confession, well then life can begin.

Sure. Joyce was an honest apostate. He does however put one in mind of Dr. Johnson's remark that the Irish are an honest race – they never speak well of one another. With Joyce, lack of charity began at home. I do not mean the way he treated his parents – they come through as poignantly sympathetic – but the way he presents himself. It is difficult to believe that he did not, in later life, see the arrogant romanticism of his youthful self. Stephen is the least attractive figure in the story.

Joyce was fated to become very much like the father he had scorned and in a lovely poem "Ecce Puer," written about the birth of his son and the death of his father, he begs the old man's forgiveness. A painting of John Joyce by Patrick Tuohy hung in Joyce's apartment; in it, the old man has the look of someone about to tell a lie, or sing a song, or ask for another drink. Like his father, Joyce drank to excess and was a sentimental parent and a sometime philandering husband, who forced his own irreligion on his wife, whom he didn't legally marry until 1931.

It is not surprising that Joyce, having been so extensively educated by them, should have considered joining the Jesuits and becoming a priest. When his faith went, he made a religion of his writing and ruthlessly sacrificed all else to it. Through years of exile, poverty, and difficulties getting published, he persisted, and eventually recognition and fame came.

The development from the *Portrait*, through *Ulysses*, to *Finnegan's Wake* is usually taken to be one of artistic advancement. Seen in another way, it is a pathological progression toward greater and greater self-absorption. The fairly straightforward autobiographical novel was followed by *Ulysses*, which takes its structure from Homer and is set on a single day, June 16, 1904, in the life of Leopold Bloom. If Ellmann, Joyce's biographer, can be trusted, the author returning from a night on the town fed into the manuscript incidents the meaning of which could be known only to Joyce or to a researcher as assiduous as Ellmann. Joyce produced a novel all but unintelligible without a commentary.

With *Finnegan's Wake*, Joyce creates a private language to go with his private universe. He had an extraordinary gift for languages, classical and modern – he earned his living as a Berlitz instructor – such that the work is the apotheosis of the view that the artist is the subject of his art.

His wife outlived him, went to Mass, said her beads, received the last sacraments. No doubt she prayed for the bibulous, skeptical, loving genius who was her husband.

MONSIGNOR GEORGE A. KELLY

Never content to be a spectator or chronicler of events, Kelly sought to counter the impression that all Catholic academics were at odds with Rome by founding the Fellowship of Catholic Scholars.

WHEN *The Battle for the American Church* appeared in 1979, it was a bombshell. Here was a detailed, careful, documented account of what had happened to the Roman Catholic Church in the United States since the close of Vatican II in 1965. There had been nothing like it before.

The sense that something was going wrong with the renewal set in motion by Vatican II was widespread. Liturgical innovations of a silly if not sacrilegious sort had become the common coin of Catholic conversation. Balloons were released, a kind of pep-rally air invaded the churches, parents were subjected to demeaning exercises by the new cadre of religious instructors coming out of graduate school with their M.Div.'s and elbowing the pastors aside. "Somewhere in this room a bag is hidden. We are all going to search for it." Thus parents were addressed when they attended the mandatory meeting if their children were to be confirmed. The idea was to suggest the notion of a gift, a surprise. Oh whoopee. People slunk home in embarrassment from such encounters, if they didn't blow their stacks. But these were minor matters.

Monsignor Kelly was not trading on the excesses or gaucheries of this priest or that nun or some director of religious education. His concern was faith and morals. If one were to select a single post-conciliar event to show how things went wrong, it would doubtless be the incredible – and incredulous – response to Paul VI's *Humanae Vitae* in 1968. Kelly's book made it clear that this was not an isolated event, nor did it spring out of nowhere. The *Battle* helped us see that noisy theological dissent and the rejection of the Church's sexual morality was part of a large sad picture.

Who was Monsignor George Kelly? Born in New York in 1916, he was ordained in 1942. After earning his Ph.D. at the Catholic University, he returned to New York to parish work but also as Family Life Director and Secretary for Education in the Archdiocese of New York. The chapter on "Learning the Church Spellman Style" in his autobiography *Inside My Father's House* (1989) provides the best insight into Kelly's conception of himself as a priest.

He has a undeniably pre-conciliar *look* about him. Always in clerical dress, with an inexhaustible fund of clerical stories, most of them involving bishops, he grew up in a Church where bishops were bishops, pastors were pastors, and laypeople were laypeople. Kelly is the quintessential Catholic priest. He is also a quintessential American. The different roles in the Church were not altered by Vatican II; they were; if anything, reinforced, but styles can change, and Kelly has no quarrel with that. Indeed, he can rightly say that he prepared the way for desirable changes through his Family Life work. The *Battle* drew attention to six alarming trends.

First, controversy over the very nature of the Church, invoking the Council as having set aside the "hierarchical" model! Second, the controversy over the renewal of Religious life. Third, the controversy over Divine Revelation. Fourth, the controversy over religious freedom in the Church. Fifth, the controversy over contraception. Sixth, the controversy over the extent of the Church's involvement in worldly affairs.

Kelly begins with the changes on the Catholic campuses of the nation, citing the Land O'Lakes Declaration of 1967 as crucial. This event has to be understood in terms of what led up to it, and

Kelly knows the story. He was involved in it every step of the way. He traces with muted dismay the decision of Catholic institutions to cut their ties with the hierarchy, to downplay their commitment to the faith, often for the sake of state aid.

By beginning with Catholic education, Monsignor Kelly not only reveals his own keen interest in it but rightly points to that which played a role in all the subsequent events he relates. Never content to be a spectator or chronicler of events, Kelly sought to counter the impression that all Catholic academics were at odds with Rome by founding the Fellowship of Catholic Scholars, which flourishes and expands with every year.

On with the lamentable litany the *Battle* continues, the Curran commotion at Catholic University, the incredible collapse in some orders of religious women. The great spiritual writers of the past gave way to Erik Erikson, the campuses nuns attended during summer school became dating bureaus, and many marriages between priests and nuns had their origin there.

Priests and nuns and laity were being told that it was an entirely new ball game. The old Church with its rules and prohibitions and fear of God was dead. Celibacy and the vow of chastity were reinterpreted. Dr. Johnson's dictum that marriage has its pains but celibacy has no pleasures lost its point. Being a Catholic was redefined into a style of life that had previously characterized non-Catholics, even anti-Catholics. Pope-bashing 501 was the point of departure of graduate studies in theology.

To this day there is no better account of the first fifteen years after the close of the council than George Kelly's *The Battle for the American Church*. Those who are new in the Church, young people wondering what all the aging dissenters are whining about, would do well to read Monsignor Kelly's account of the struggle that continues in the Church in the United States.

Prior to his retirement, Kelly's base was St. John's University on Long Island. A stream of books appeared, some analyzing the situation we are in, others mapping out the way we should go. He wrote on biblical scholarship, he reminded the bishops of their responsibility for what is going on, he lobbied, cajoled, and nurtured the Fellowship into the powerful voice for orthodoxy it has become.

"In the next century is the U.S. Catholic Church to reflect as essential elements of its nature the definitions and norms proclaimed by John Paul II, or will it be a Church which officially accepts 'pick-and-choose Catholicism' as an approved opinion for its constituency?"

Those are the stakes, as he put it in *Keeping the Church Catholic with John Paul II* (1990). It is important that we realize this. It is important that we act in the light of the realization. The work of Monsignor George A. Kelly, his books and his legacy, have made this considerably easier for us to do.

JACQUES MARITAIN

That the pursuit of intellectual knowledge goes hand in hand with the spiritual life is the key to seeing Maritain as the model for the Catholic thinker.

NOT long ago I drove from Strasbourg to the little town of Kolbsheim, so little it wasn't even on my map, and to its little cemetery where Jacques Maritain lies in the same grave as his wife Raïssa. The Chateau in Kolbsheim, of which Antoinette Grunelius is chatelaine, houses the Cercle d'études Jacques et Raïssa Maritain, which is just now bringing to completion its magnificent fifteen-volume edition of the *Oeuvres Complétes*. I had come to talk with René Mougel about the launching of the twenty-volume Notre Dame edition of the works of Maritain in English and of ways in which the Jacques Maritain Center at Notre Dame could cooperate with the Cercle d'études.

Standing at the grave with René, praying for the repose of the souls of Jacques and his wife, but also asking their support for the work to be undertaken, I marveled at how Raïssa's memoirs had made so many of us feel part of their circle of friends. *We Have Been Friends Together* and *Adventures in Grace* were written in wartime in New York where they were in exile from occupied France. It is all but impossible to write of one Maritain without writing of the other, but I shall concentrate now on Jacques and subsequently write on Raïssa.

Born in Paris in 1882, Jacques Maritain entered the Catholic Church in 1906, along with Raïssa, his wife since 1904, and her sister Vera, whose life was intertwined with the Maritains. The writer Leon Bloy, who became their godfather, was instrumental in their conversion, but prior to that the lectures of Henri Bergson, to which Maritain had been led by Charles Peguy, were a disposing cause.

After his conversion, Maritain studied biology for two years in Heidelberg. It was not until 1910 that Jacques published his first article; that very year he began the study of St. Thomas Aquinas, something Raïssa had already done. Maritain was to become one of the greatest leaders of the Thomistic Revival envisaged by Leo XIII in his encyclical *Aeterni Patris* in 1879, three years before Jacques was born. The encyclical *Pascendi* issued by Pius X set the tone of Maritain's work. One of his early books was entitled *Antimodern.*

The range of Maritain's philosophical interests alone amazes. Like his mentor Thomas Aquinas, he took philosophy to be whatever we can come to know by our natural powers. From the beginning of his career, he was concerned with the relation of science to other branches of philosophy. In his masterpiece, *The Degrees of Knowledge*, he sets forth an ordered panorama of wisdoms, from natural science through metaphysics and theology to that wisdom that is the gift of the Holy Ghost. That the pursuit of intellectual knowledge goes hand in hand with the spiritual life is the key to seeing Maritain as the model for the Catholic thinker (as his wife may be seen as a model of the Catholic artist).

After World War I, the Maritains inaugurated their Thomistic Study Circles, inviting philosophers, artists, writers, poets, theologians. These gatherings were as much retreats as conferences. In his *Note-Book*, published in 1965, Maritain both described the Thomistic Circle and reproduced its Statutes.

According primacy is the fact that the Church has recommended Thomas Aquinas as our mentor in philosophy and theology. The task of thinker and artist is to make felt in his work that union of faith and reason defended so vigorously by Thomas.

Equally important is the recognition that the divorce of the intellectual or artistic life from prayer will lead to chaos, in the life of the person and in his work.

The growing role of lay people in fulfilling the aims of the Thomistic revival is underscored.

Jacques and Raïssa had already expressed these thoughts in a jointly authored book called, in translation, *Prayer and Intelligence*. It was out of a rich spiritual life that the works of Jacques Maritain came. His major lesson for today lies here, I think. There is a danger of putting the life of the mind and imagination on one side and the life of faith on the other. Knowledge and culture are presumed to be secular, spiritually neutral, while the practice of the faith becomes increasingly emotional and devoid of specific doctrinal content.

This separation is taking place before our eyes in Catholic institutions of higher learning, which seem alarmed at the suggestion that the faith is relevant to what goes on in classroom and lab and not simply in the chapels. The Statutes of the Thomistic Circles point to the danger of that kind of divorce, and in doing so they consciously echo the long tradition of Catholic spirituality.

It is not simply that moral virtues must govern the activities thinkers and artists engage in; the faith is internally important in every activity engaged in by the believer. Thomism for Maritain was a specific content but it was also a name for something incumbent on all. "Woe is me if I should not follow Thomas" is not the slogan of a fan, but a wise man's recognition of that in Thomas which is greater than Thomas.

The convert more than the cradle Catholic recognizes the responsibility to draw others to the faith. Maritain was a legendary convert maker in person, but his writings have functioned in the stories of many conversions. So too his writings on aesthetics, *Art and Scholasticism* and *Creative Intuition in Art and Poetry*, have influenced many writers and artists and poets.

For almost twenty years of his life, the forties and fifties, Maritain was closely associated with this country, residing here during much of those two decades. In *Reflections on America*, he set down his somewhat uncritical affection for the United States.

When Raïssa died in 1960, Jacques left Princeton for France, settling in Toulouse, where he taught novices of the Little Brothers of Jesus. He was into his nineties when he died, and toward the end he took the habit of a Little Brother.

Maritain served as France's ambassador to the Vatican for several years after World War II and represented his country when UNESCO was founded. His political philosophy has always kept his followers on their toes. It is only ideologues who are predictable, and Maritain was constantly surprising his friends. Initially close to *l'Action Française* he moved to the left with *Integral Humanism*, but his later appreciation of America surprised some. But it was his *Peasant of the Garonne* of 1966 that turned Catholic progressives against him. Maritain was the first to discern and to warn against bogus uses of Vatican II.

There are two international Maritain groups, an American Maritain Society, the new uniform edition of his works and the forthcoming Notre Dame edition. His greatest influence still lies ahead as more and more find themselves saying with Raïssa, "We have been friends together."

RAÏSSA MARITAIN

When Raïssa was nineteen and Jacques twenty, they resolved to commit suicide if they did not within a year find some reason for living.

RAÏSSA Oumansov was born in Russia on August 31, 1883, into a Jewish family. Her extraordinary talents were early apparent, and their recognition played a role in the family's decision to emigrate. Their goal was New York, but they settled in France, and here Raïssa flourished even more, intellectually, although she drifted from the religious practices of her family. Yet, when asked in her baccalaureate examination in philosophy what she wished to learn, she replied, "To know what is, monsieur." She entered the Sorbonne at seventeen, a very good year. It was then that she met Jacques Maritain.

For sixty years, from 1900 until 1960 when Raïssa died, she and Jacques seemed but two sides of the same coin, perfect complements to one another. She was the mystic, the poet, the eternal feminine; he was the scientist, the philosopher, eventually the theologian. He called her *dimidium animae meae*, half my soul. It was not that the one lacked what the other had, but rather that some things predominated in her and others in him.

When they met, each a student of science, they had both abandoned the religion of their families. Jacques came from Protestant stock; though his father had been a non-practicing Catholic, he was now agnostic. In their studies they found nothing that answered to their deep-seated desire for comprehensive answers. There are questions we associate with the young because they have not yet become dulled to them. What does it all mean? What is the point of human effort in a vast and seemingly impersonal universe? When Raïssa was nineteen and Jacques twenty, they resolved to commit suicide if they did not within a year find some reason for living.

In a time when mystifying teenage suicides abound, with motivations apparently of the most banal, we may miss the seriousness of the resolution this young couple made at the beginning of the century. Fortunately they found the only answer to that great Why. They began to read a writer whom they had never met, certainly not an ordinary or indeed successful writer. His name was Leon Bloy. His novel, *The Woman Who Was Poor* ended with the haunting sentence, "There is but one tragedy, not to be a saint." They went to see Bloy.

Earlier, following the lectures of Henri Bergson, the Maritains had been eased somewhat from materialism, but with Bloy they found a robust exponent of the belief that the drama of a human life is played out against an eternal background. Bloy was, they felt, a pilgrim of the Absolute. In his life, the salvation offered by faith in Jesus Christ and in his Church, was the paramount fact. Beside that, nothing else mattered. The young Maritains were overwhelmed. They helped him financially – he was as desperately poor as the heroine of his novel –, they came again and again; eventually the grace of faith was given them, and they entered the Church on June 11, 1906, along with Raïssa's sister Vera. Their godfather? Leon Bloy.

The devotion of Raïssa's older sister Vera had begun when they were children in Russia. When Raïssa married Jacques and they went off to Heidelberg where Jacques studied biology for two years, Vera joined them. She would be with them to the end of her days.

If Jacques and Raïssa came into the Church together, she was to take the lead in several ways. From the beginning, Raïssa felt drawn to the fullness of the spiritual life, to mysticism, to contemplation. Moreover, she was the first to read St. Thomas Aquinas and to urge the Angelic Doctor on Jacques. Jacques was destined to become the leading Thomist of his time, to develop the principles of Thomas and to apply them and expand them in ways undreamt of by Thomas himself. To be a Thomist was not to cultivate the thought of the past, but to make fruitful in the present eternal truths.

Back in France, Jacques became engaged in editorial work and then in teaching, but their friendships show the influence of Raïssa. Artists, writers, poets, and thinkers began to congregate around them. Entering whole-heartedly into Catholic life, they wanted both to live it to the fullest – early on they acquired a Dominican spiritual director – and to share it with others. They were influential in the coming back to the faith of many nominal Catholics and the conversion of others.

The founding of the Thomistic Study Circle in 1920 was a natural development which reflected the union of the intellectual and spiritual the Maritains had expressed in *La vie d'oraison*, translated as *Prayer and Intelligence*. If the pursuits of truth and beauty do not spring from a life of prayer, they cannot effectively attain their ends. How odd this sounds to our secularized ears. Yet it was a message to which many thinkers and artists responded.

Recently in Paris, I stopped in at the little side chapel in Saint-Severin, where daily Mass is said. On the chapel walls was an exhibition of drawings of Rouault, an artist whose connection with the Maritains was stressed in the notes for the exhibition. The religious themes of the painter were appropriate for the setting. Roualt was only one of the artists who found in the Maritains an inspiration that had something to do with the Holy Spirit.

In 1940, when France fell to the Germans, the Maritains were in this country, and it was here they spent the war years. Their anguish at the fate of their country, their nostalgia for it, led Raïssa to write, almost therapeutically, her memoirs. *We Have Been Friends Together* and *Adventures in Grace* recall their friendships and the special nature of their relations to others. These memoirs put a generation of Americans in touch with a world they had never known, friends they had never had, in a way that suggested a relevance beyond the Maritains.

Raïssa wrote far less than Jacques, but then that was not her dominant vocation. Hers was more appropriate to her sex. Indeed her views on the differences between men and women struck a recent biographer as old-fashioned and "quasi-fundamentalist." They certainly are out of step with current trends, but then hers is the perennial outlook. Women would do well to reflect on what she has to say to them about the feminine.

The loss of Raïssa in 1960 was cruelly hard for Jacques, who had thirteen more years to live. In 1963 he published her journals, along with a number of occasional writings. For Jacques, the preparation of these for publication was a labor of love. She is revealed to us as a woman of contemplative and mystical depth, whose understanding of poetry – she herself was a poet – is profound. She wrote of poetry as a spiritual experience, a phrase with a determinate meaning in her usage. But it is perhaps the short texts on prayer, on the relation of God to men, and on Christ that engage the reader more.

In 1973, Jacques joined the other half of his soul. They share a common grave in Kolbsheim.

FRANÇOIS MAURIAC

All in all, there are more sinners than saints in his stories and, as his statement indicates, it is the subtle, inward betrayals that interest him.

In the days when Catholics had a livelier sense of their co-religionists in other countries, François Mauriac would have shown up on anyone's short list of great Catholic novelists. Far from being resigned to the marginal status to which the WASP domination might have wished for them, American Catholics were at home in the larger mainstream of Western culture. They felt kinship with French novelists, English artists, German thinkers like Karl Adam and Josef Pieper, and a host of other writers and artists in many countries whose work was animated by the faith that had produced European culture.

Born (1885), raised, and educated in Bordeaux, François Mauriac went to Paris at the age of twenty, where he enrolled in the École de Chartes. It is possible to imagine Mauriac as a paleographer, living out his days poring over manuscripts, breathing the dust of libraries. He was an aesthete, uneasy with the working classes, capable of the careful, unrewarding work of the scholar. But that was not to be. After a year, Mauriac altered his plans: he would become an artist. The world is a better place for that decision. His first book was a collection of his poems.

Many efforts have been made to discern Mauriac's political beliefs. It is certain that as a young man he was close to the right, to the royalists represented by Action Française whose leader Charles Maurras was an agnostic who thought of Catholicism as a bulwark of social order. The movement had begun as a response to the Dreyfus case and had an anti-Semitic tinge.

Action Française was condemned by Rome in 1926, something that annoyed many Catholics but permitted others to separate themselves from a political movement that treated the faith cynically.

It can be argued that it was not the politics but the affirmation of traditional morality and its emphasis on the family that attracted Mauriac to the right. His early novels display the tensions within the family - a son oppressed by his mother, a daughter-in-law who is acquitted of poisoning her husband, the brood of vipers who gather like crows while the patriarch dies. Not a pretty picture.

Mauriac's novels take place in half-light, his characters are troubled and by and large joyless, their Catholicism is a judgment on them. *A Kiss for the Leper*, *Viper's Tangle*, *The Desert of Love*, *Thérèse* were perhaps the ones most familiar to Americans. What was he up to as a novelist?

"If there is a reason for the existence of the novelist on earth it is this: to show the element which holds out against God in the highest and noblest characters - the innermost evils and dissimulations; and also to light up the secret sources of sanctity in creatures which seem to us to have failed."

All in all, there are more sinners than saints in his stories and, as his statement indicates, it is the subtle, inward betrayals that interest him. To call his novels psychological would be wrong, given what that term tends nowadays to mean. Mauriac is interested in the drama of salvation, the deeds whereby human agents decide their eternal lot, not supposedly exonerating subconscious mechanisms.

In photographs from youth to old age, Mauriac is a thin figure with a massive nose and large heavy-lidded tragic eyes. When he is not collapsed in a chair, he stands like a carpenter's ruler that has not been completely unfolded. Frail, fragile, pallid, he seems an unlikely man to have produced the passion of the stories. Not a barrel of laughs, one suspects, but for all that a writer of power and pointilistic precision in depicting the gradations of good and evil in his characters.

Geoffrey Chaucer, late in his life, published a Retraction in which he expressed regret for having written what he had, including the *Canterbury Tales*, because he feared they were occasions of sin for the reader. Mauriac, stung by the shocked reaction of fellow Catholics (as well as by André Gide's jibe that he sought permission to be a Christian without having to burn his books), entertained similar misgivings about his novels.

In 1928, he went through a religious crisis from which he emerged resolved to be an unequivocally Catholic writer. There are critics who consider moral or religious convictions an impediment to the artist, no matter the centuries when almost every great artist was a Christian. But narrative art does pose problems of the kind that bother writers as responsible as Chaucer and Mauriac, and they are to be admired for appreciating the inescapable moral implications of art.

Jacques Maritain had argued that the novelist who would depict sin must have the sanctity of St. Augustine. If observed, this rule would lead to a perhaps welcome reduction in the number of novelists, but it is clearly an overstatement. Generally speaking, the writer should get no more blame for the evil of his characters than he gets credit for their heroism.

Mauriac wrote a number of books which deal with the peculiar problems of the writer. *God and Mammon* (1929) was written in response to Gide's taunt. Ten years later, at the beginning of the German occupation of France, Mauriac wrote *Woman of the Pharisees* in response to a dismissing remark of Jean-Paul Sartre's. Mauriac had compared the relation of the writer to his characters with God's to his creatures. Sartre, an atheist, retorted that God was no artist, and neither was Mauriac.

Mauriac had been elected to the French Academy in 1933, he was universally acknowledged as a great writer, but he was stung by what Sartre had written. The response was a novel of great accomplishment - and almost unalleviated evil in the main character. No unbeliever could have been harder on Catholic characters than Mauriac.

There was a Jansenist streak in him, a tendency to see evil as an almost dominant force. His characters are unattractive, physically and spiritually, by and large, riddled with one or another of the capital sins. It is as if Dante never made it out of the Inferno. Mauriac himself felt this and, having nearly died after the appearance of *Brood of Vipers*, published *The Frontenac Mystery* in 1932, in which a happy and virtuous family is put before us.

Mauriac played a major part in the revival of Catholic letters in France, which we associate with Peguy and Claudel and Bernanos. The Nobel Prize added global recognition to his inclusion among the immortals of the French Academy. He was interested in the work of Graham Greene, and vice versa. The latter's *Heart of the Matter* poses some of the problems apparently found in *Thérèse*, the sinner qua sinner being justified.

To his countrymen, Mauriac was a journalist as well as a man of letters, and he was to become an enthusiastic supporter of Charles de Gaulle. Mauriac's *Bloc Notes* and his *Memoirs* require a good deal of knowledge of the specifically French political landscape in order to be understood. But the novels retain their immediacy and pay rich rewards to the reader.

THOMAS MERTON

One of the oddities of Merton's autobiography was the suggestion that the Trappist life wasn't demanding enough. Maybe if war-time conditions had not prevented it, he would have entered a Carthusian monastery.

Thomas Merton's autobiography, *The Seven Storey Mountain*, appeared in 1948, when its author was thirty-three years old. It told the story of a young man who, from no religion at all, became a Catholic, thought of entering the Franciscans, and then, at the age of twenty-six, entered the Order of Cistercians of the Strict Observance – the Trappists – at Gethsemani Abbey in Kentucky.

Merton was born in France in 1915 of a New Zealand father, who was an artist, and an American mother, but he was orphaned early. He was raised in France, in England, in the United States, and, in the years preceding his conversion, was an aspiring writer, political radical, campus cut-up, and vagabond lover.

When his book appeared, in the years after World War II, the campuses were swarming with veterans whose war-time experiences had aged if not matured them; Merton spoke with the authority of someone who had done everything you had, and maybe more, and, in the great tradition of religious conversion, had then done a 180-degree turn and become a monk, determined to be a saint.

The impact of this book on young Catholics, and not only them, in this country cannot be overestimated. Merton gave voice to the longing for contemplation which is latent in any human heart. He put before one a spiritual and ascetic ideal that went against the grain of the age – as it has gone against the grain of every age. Following the story of his life that had led him to a monastery in rural Kentucky, readers saw possibilities in their own lives that might otherwise have escaped them. Merton provided a dramatic meditation on the unavoidable question: What is the point and meaning of a human life?

It is not too much to say that, more than anyone else, Thomas Merton was responsible for the amazing growth of the Trappist Order in this country. New foundations sprang up across the country and were quickly filled with eager novices.

I was an undergraduate when I read Merton's autobiography and its impact on me was indelible, although not in every way the one he wished to make. The description of his efforts to write and publish novels fascinated me almost as much as the description of his religious vocation. That he and his friends would spend the summer in a rented cottage, plugging away at their novels, titillated my imagination. Later, in 1969, one of Merton's failed novels would be printed: *My Argument with the Gestapo: A Macaronic Journal*. It was difficult to avoid the thought that he would have starved as a novelist. He was a better poet, and indeed collections of his poems were published by New Directions before the autobiography appeared.

And here lay one of the great ironies of his life. When he entered the Trappists, he put behind him all his secular ambitions, including that of becoming a writer, yet he was destined to become a world-famous author as a Trappist, though he published under his secular name. It was not his idea to write as a monk, but when he was asked to do so, he went at it with great gusto, and books flowed out of Gethsemani until he died in 1968 at the age of fifty-three – indeed, the flow continued after his death. His range was enormous, and he had a knack of making an immediate contact with his reader, speaking with the voice of an older brother, a spiritual director, someone like and unlike.

One of the oddities of Merton's autobiography was the suggestion that the Trappist life wasn't demanding enough. Maybe if war-time conditions had not prevented it, he would have entered a Carthusian monastery. A lifelong tension between the cenobitic and hermetic ideals of monasticism began, and Merton would eventually argue that the Trappists themselves were originally meant to be more hermetic than cenobitic. In any case, he was permitted to build a hermitage in the woods of the monastery and to spend increasing amounts of time alone. It was in the hermitage that John Howard Griffin took the famous photographs of Jacques Maritain and Merton. I used the hermitage for a scene in my novel *The Noonday Devil*.

The two essential biographies of Merton are by Monica Furlong and by Michael Mott. We learn something Merton had been advised to leave out of *The Seven Storey Mountain*. As a student in England, he had a child, but the boy and his mother were later killed during the air raids on London. This underscores Merton's sense that he entered the monastery to do penance for his past life.

The biographies disturb our sense that, when Merton entered the monastery, the old life was left behind and a new one, the one that produced *Seeds of Contemplation* and a whole series of books depicting advancement in the spiritual life, began. Life, even monastic life, is never that simple. It seems inescapable that Merton's abbot came to find him a pain in the neck, and not without reason. Merton felt he was unfairly dealt with, but it is easy to be struck by how patiently the abbot and his fellow monks endured Merton's idiosyncrasies.

The literary life beyond the walls invaded the monastic redoubt. The hermitage seemed less, rather than more, demanding than community life. Reading of Merton working there, listening to Joan Baez records, drinking wine, we might think that at the time we were more monkish than our favorite monkish mentor. He had visitors. He engaged in a vast and global correspondence. His interest in political matters grew, and he allied himself with anti-war and pacifist groups. Increasingly, he romanticized such involvements, calling his missive to the outside world *Cables from the Ace* and *Reflections of a Guilty Bystander*.

Merton's interest in Eastern mysticism grew and took on odd dimensions. Nor was he spared the temptations of the flesh.

Mott tells us of Merton, in hospital in Louisville, falling in love with a nurse and ready to desert his vocation and marry her. That he did not owed more to her maturity than his.

Frankly, I was shocked when I read of this faltering, but on reflection I have come to think that it is an essential element in Merton's influence. We lay people are wont to make impossible demands on the clergy and religious, as if they were already *in patria* rather than *in via* with the rest of us. There is something pharisaical in our surprise that even those who have given their lives to the quest of perfection often fall short. No doubt it would have been better if Merton had not suffered this foolish lapse in Louisville. But it should not obscure the fact that, despite it, in some ways because of it, he hung in there and was true to the vocation to which he had been called.

He died in Bangkok, electrocuted by a faulty connection, and was returned to Gethsemani for burial. The immortality he sought was not that of authorship, but his books will go on doing good for many for a long time to come. In part this is due to the devotion of his admirers, who have refused to let obscurity claim him.

Brother Patrick Hart, a fellow Trappist who served as secretary to Merton, has earned the gratitude of us all for his self-effacing and tireless effort to keep the flame alight. Brother Patrick has edited the letters of Merton and brought together his literary essays. But his monument will surely be the seven volumes of Merton's journals, of which he is the general editor.

Several volumes have already been published: *Run to the Mountain, 1939–1941*, edited by Brother Patrick, and *Entering the Silence, 1941–1952*, edited by Jonathan Montaldo. Future volumes will be edited by Christine Bochen, Lawrence Cunningham, Robert Daggy, and Victor Kramer. Brother Patrick himself will edit the final volume. The journals have been mined for particular publications, the main story of Merton's life is known, but the complete journals will deepen our understanding of this remarkable man, *notre semblable, notre frere.*

When I first read *Seven Storey Mountain*, in the year of its appearance, I was overwhelmed and somewhat shamed by the freshness and awe with which Merton spoke of things which had become matter-of-fact to me. Doubtless the convert will always open the eyes of the cradle Catholic to the marvels he takes for granted. But it was Merton's enthusiasm for Catholic culture, particularly the spiritual and intellectual patrimony of the Church, that awoke in me a desire to assimilate and be grateful for that great tradition.

Was Merton a good poet? I am no judge, of course, but he does seem uneven to me. He wrote free verse, tennis without a net, but sometimes it worked. Often it did not, and his similes would not cohere. Oddly, the failures happened when he was under the influence of the Psalms.

His continuing role is that of a spiritual type, a gifted author of protreptic works that awaken a deep longing for the inner life. The complete journals will give us the man, warts and all. Perhaps, as with the de-saccharinizing of the Little Flower, this will make him even more appealing to *l'homme moyen sensuel*. Mount's biography shocked me a little and I indulged some pharisaical thoughts. Any flaw in someone striving for sanctity sets off the hum of criticism in those of us who could not have lived a day of the life to which Thomas Merton gave twenty-seven years of his. It is good to settle down again with this marvelous and saintly author.

BRIAN MOORE

A Catholic, often a priest, losing his faith has become the trademark of Brian Moore's fiction. There are other recurrences – someone in the hotel business, a failed poet, surprising mothers, some of the most believable women characters in contemporary fiction – but it is the loosening grip on faith that provides Moore with the theme of most of his novels.

In *The Lonely Passion of Judith Hearne*, published in 1956, Brian Moore gave us an unforgettably moving portrait of a Belfast spinster whose life is a downward spiral of misfortune due to plain looks, a domineering aunt, and alcohol. It is when doubts against her faith are added to envy and surreptitious sipping that the story reaches its climax. Judith, drunk, doubtful that Jesus resides sacramentally behind the closed doors of the tabernacle, reels into the sanctuary and up the altar steps and tries ineffectually to pry open the tabernacle.

This was Brian Moore's first novel. One of his most recent, *No Other Life*, set in what most readers will imagine as Haiti, concerns a black priest who rises to the presidency while the narrator, his white mentor, a Canadian priest, loses his faith and, in the words of the title, concludes that there is no other life than this one. It is to Moore's artistic credit that the lone alternative to eternal life is stark, violent, and irrational.

A Catholic, often a priest, losing his faith has become the trademark of Brian Moore's fiction. There are other recurrences – someone in the hotel business, a failed poet, surprising mothers, some of the most believable women characters in contemporary fiction – but it is the loosening grip on faith that provides Moore with the theme of most of his novels. Aspects of his own ambiguous national identity are also frequent.

A native of Belfast who emigrated to Canada – where his fiction career began – but has long lived in California (see *Fergus*, 1970), Moore still seems most imaginatively at home in an Irish background. His antepenultimate novel, *Lies of Silence* (1990), set in an authoritatively evoked Belfast, is perhaps the most plotted of his stories, yet it retains the looked-for Moore interiorization of the action plot that turns a thriller into a drama of moral victory in defeat.

We are not surprised to learn that Brian Moore's heroes read, among other favorite authors, Graham Greene. In the Irish as in the English author, there is a persistent rivalry between lust and religious practices, with the latter, and the faith that sustains them, eventually eclipsed by adulterous liaisons. Equally, there is a refusal to allow sexual self-indulgence to rise much above the sordid. Religion may be shuffled off, but untroubled liberation is not the result; rather there is a concatenation of disastrous effects that almost seem an argument for chastity, if not indeed celibacy.

The moonscape power of Moore's fiction lies precisely here. The loss of faith is loss indeed, and it is often taken to have Dostoevskian consequences. If God does not exist, anything goes. But there is a residual decency in his characters which prevents them from taking, save in evanescent fantasy, a nihilist route.

In *Lies of Silence*, Michael Dillon endangers the life of the wife he longs to leave by saving hundreds from an IRS bomb, leaves his wife and Ireland with a young BBC woman whose attractions seem largely those of a sexual acrobat, dissociates himself from his wife's highly public defiance of the terrorists, vacillates between giving testimony against one of the terrorists, and then, having decided on the only honorable course. . . . Well, there then follows an ending that only a serious writer would dare to write.

I know nothing more about Brian Moore than what can be gleaned from the dust jackets of his novels. This is in many ways refreshing: he is a writer content to let his writings speak for him.

In the age of the literary self-promoter – when a proven dud like Norman Mailer, weary of comparing himself to Hemingway, now courts the Nobel Prize which, one can safely say, is just about what he deserves – in such an age, the artistic self-effacement of Brian Moore is refreshing. It is also tantalizing. Who is the author of these novels in which Catholics regularly lose their faith? All we need really know is that they are stories of rare integrity in which, as Graham Greene rightly observed, the author does not intrude. It is difficult to imagine his characters acting otherwise than as they do, however surprising their acts may seem.

His first novel is told from several viewpoints, not only that of Judith Hearne, but when the heroine is on stage the reader becomes an unmarried shabby-genteel Irishwoman in her early forties, desperate and tipsy because life is passing her by. Ten years later, in *I Am Mary Dunne* (1966), Moore wrote a first-person novel through the viewpoint of his title character, yet at no time is the reader conscious of what a remarkable *tour de force* this is. *The Temptation of Eileen Hughes* (1981) proved that this uncanny capacity to occupy the female psyche is a matter of art, not luck.

It was the futuristic novella *Catholics* (1972), which became a very effective teleplay with Martin Sheen, that made Moore's fiction known to many – though, in the manner of television, more or less anonymously; after all, he was only the author. The story has all the Brian Moore staples as well as a treatment only he could have provided. The contrast between the old Church of Muck Abbey – the Albanesian Order reappears in Moore's latest novel – and Father Kinsella, on a mission from the World Council of Churches to inquire into the strange orthodoxy of the monks, seems to promise one kind of story, but we get something quite different from the conflict of old and new. The only conflicts Brian Moore is genuinely interested in are within the soul, and they concern the person and his faith, or lack of it.

In *Black Robe* (1985) and *The Color of Blood* (1987), Moore returned to the troubled cleric, in the former a French Jesuit missionary to the Hurons, in the latter a contemporary Eastern

European Cardinal. But the familiarity of the theme should not blind us to the truly virtuoso performances in these novels.

Brian Moore's reader, one who has followed his novels over the years, might reasonably assume that the author is a disenchanted lapsed Catholic. But he might with equal reasonableness assume that the author is one whose Catholicism has never lost him. Whatever the biographical truth, the artistic truth is that the imagination of Brian Moore is inseparable from Roman Catholicism. In that sense, surely, he is a Catholic author and one of enormous power and achievement.

EDWIN O'CONNOR

O'Connor himself never created a character he didn't love. Indeed, it can often be said of him what John Updike said of J. P. Salinger: not even God could love his characters as much as he does.

Edwin O'Connor (1918–1968) wrote three widely read novels, but he is all but identified as the author of one of them. The three novels are *The Last Hurrah* (1956), *The Edge of Sadness* (1961), and *All in the Family* (1966). These were bracketed by an early novel, *The Oracle* (1951) and by the lesser later efforts *Benjy* (1957) and *I Was Dancing* (1964).

O'Connor was born in Providence but was raised in Woonsocket, Rhode Island. His decision to go to Notre Dame was crucial for him as a writer. There he came under the charismatic influence of Frank O'Malley, to whom he would dedicate *The Edge of Sadness*. The English Department of those days was a remarkable place, particularly for a young man harboring hopes of becoming a writer. John T. Frederick and Father Leo L. Ward were there, as well as the short story writer and novelist Richard Sullivan. O'Malley was not himself a writer, but he saw imaginative literature in a way that went far beyond the vision even of his colleagues. Fiction was not merely a diversion, an opportunity for the writer to impose his ego on the reader. Rather it was seen in terms of a philosophy of Catholic culture.

It may well be that Frank O'Malley became known beyond the Notre Dame campus largely because of his influence on Edwin O'Connor. I have vivid memories of the tall shy O'Connor moving rapidly down corridors and across the campus walks when he returned for his annual visit with his old mentor. Shyness called to shyness, as the psalmist did not say, and Frank was justifiably proud of his old student, now a famous if self-effacing author.

Notre Dame in the late 1930s was both more Catholic and more Irish than it is today, and it may well be that O'Connor first became aware of himself as an Irish Catholic during his four years in South Bend. It was only when he wrote out of that lived awareness that he wrote well. The temptation to do otherwise, to assume some transcendent American persona, is one every writer feels and ought to resist.

American literature has sprung up in the most unlikely places, Mississippi River towns, the middle border of Hamlin Garland, Oak Park, St. Paul, the Tidewater Basin; it has come out of Nebraska and Indiana and out of the South. It is an amazing and various thing, yet in the hands of critics and professors there grew up the notion that it had everything to do with New England and Protestantism. It is odd to see the way William Dean Howells had to be credentialed in Boston and then New York, as if he were something other than the person he shows us in *Boy's Town*. Even Mark Twain lived out his life in the East.

There was tension, in short, between the homogenized view of the mainstream of American literature and the varied impulses out of which that literature had actually come. For a Catholic writer, there seemed to be the choice of adopting a secularized or WASP outlook, or writing for a sectarian audience. Until only a few decades ago, there was a self-contained tradition of Catholic publishing houses and Catholic fiction. Was Edwin O'Connor the first American Catholic writer to be taken on his own terms? He was certainly one of the first.

The Last Hurrah, as everybody knows, is about Irish-Catholic politicians in Boston, the last campaign of Mayor Frank Skeffington. Here is the Boston dreaded by the brahmins in John P. Marquand's novels – not only have the Irish applied, they are now accepting applications for patronage jobs in the city they have seized. O'Connor's hero was based on Mayor James Michael

Curley, and the novel is studded with stage Irishmen, grotesques of the kind that the non-Irish love to hate. It is an interesting question how much of the popularity of O'Connor's novel depended on its unintentionally feeding the anti-Irish and anti-Catholic prejudices of the reader. O'Connor himself never created a character he didn't love. Indeed, it can often be said of him what John Updike said of J. P. Salinger: not even God could love his characters as much as he does.

In *The Last Hurrah*, O'Connor moves toward what will characterize his writing, a narrator who is and is not a participant in the action narrated. Adam Caulfield, Skeffington's nephew, is not the narrator, but he provides a point of view on the action that is not completely engaged. In *The Edge of Sadness* and *All in the Family*, O'Connor writes in the first person, and the voice is all but identical in the two books, as if it is the author himself we are hearing.

O'Connor's narrative voice is at once the strength and the weakness of his writing. On the one hand, the narrator is so discursive and oblique and apologetic that the reader can become impatient; on the other hand, the tone is mesmerizing and coaxes us out of our ordinary existence into the world of the novel. Catching the attention of the reader, getting him into the imaginative events of the story, has become an increasingly difficult thing to do. The attention span of readers is influenced by the kaleidoscope of images on the screen, exacerbated now by the sensory and sensuous assault that is by no means confined to MTV.

O'Connor's technique is not that of P. G. Wodehouse, whose Oldest Member buttonholes us on the veranda of the country club to tell us a story, a story within a story, so to say. O'Connor is politely and urgently bringing to our attention events whose meaning will not be delivered up in our first response to them. O'Connor wants to meditate on the events he presents, to draw out their meaning, to share with us his sense of the *lacrimae rerum*. His first novel, *The Oracle*, dealt with a dreadful figure from the days of radio, but O'Connor could not leave the man simply as a villain. He gets beneath the skin of Christopher Usher, and our tendency to condemn begins to involve reflection on our selves. This is true of O'Connor's Frank Skeffington as well. It is not that we wish to praise and celebrate Skeffington, but O'Connor has an uncanny knack for enabling us to see ourselves in the flawed character of the mayor.

This, more than anything else, separates O'Connor from a recent type of Catholic novelist, who caters to the secularist reader by suggesting to him that all his worst fears about Catholicism are true. But caricatures of nuns and priests do not disguise the essential message: the Church is condemned because She stands athwart the moral relativism of the time. When guilt is passed off as a negative psychological state we can be sure that the sense of sin is absent. And without sin there is no Christianity.

The Edge of Sadness is one of the best novels on the priesthood ever written. *All in the Family* was taken to be based on the Kennedys, which is nonsense, but explainable no doubt because of the earlier use of James Curley as a model (John F. Kennedy succeeded Curley to the U.S. House of Representatives from the Massachusetts 11th Congressional District).

The novels of Edwin O'Connor are still easily found. Paperback editions multiply. O'Connor is a Catholic novelist who for that reason has a universal appeal.

FLANNERY O'CONNOR
Georgia Girl

"Everybody who has read Wise Blood thinks I'm a hillbilly nihilist, whereas I would like to create the impression over the television that I'm a hillbilly Thomist."

"Later he saw Jesus move from tree to tree in the back of his mind, a wild ragged figure motioning him to turn around and come off into the dark where he was not sure of his footing, where he might be walking on the water and not know it and then suddenly know it and drown."

The mind in question is that of Hazel Motes, the central figure in Flannery O'Connor's *Wise Blood*, who can stand for all her characters who are haunted by Christ and convey to the reader the wild mystery of the human person.

Flannery O'Connor lived less than forty years (1925–1964), published two short novels and two collections of short stories, and is by general consent one of the great American writers of the 20th century. A sign of this was the inclusion of her Collected Works in the prestigious Library of America.

A cradle Catholic, she was more concerned than most Catholic authors about the relationship between her fiction and her faith. In retrospect, we can see that Flannery O'Connor was a beneficiary of the Catholic culture that flourished prior to the Second Vatican Council. She also experienced annoyances from that culture.

"Everybody who has read *Wise Blood* thinks I'm a hillbilly nihilist, whereas I would like to create the impression over the television that I'm a hillbilly Thomist." This is not merely a quip.

A book that exercised a great influence on O'Connor was Jacques Maritain's *Art and Scholasticism*.

Nowadays many Catholic intellectuals would be embarrassed by the unabashed scholasticism of Maritain's little work. Even a fan of it would admit that it is pretty heavy on block quotes from St. Thomas Aquinas and that the view of art it conveys is as old as Aristotle. A later Maritain developed a mystical notion of the experience of the artist as a connatural affinity with reality, but there is nothing so fancy as that in the work that influenced O'Connor. On the other hand, she had a surprising weakness for Teilhard de Chardin.

When Flannery O'Connor read *Art and Scholasticism*, she had been to the Iowa Writer's School, where she learned many things and certainly developed as a writer. But one of the banes of creative-writing courses is that they convey the notion that writing is self-expression. Flannery O'Connor felt no desire to express herself. That is why when she encountered the Aristotelian-Thomist conception of art in Maritain; she welcomed it as far truer to what she was engaged in.

Art, Aristotle said, is knowing how to make things well. The well-made thing, the story carefully wrought so as to convey what the writer wants it to convey, the perfected artifact – that is the aim of art. This is the truth that freed Flannery O'Connor from the suffocating notion that the writer's primary subject is the writer himself.

This is not to say that the quite distinctive voice of Flannery O'Connor is not audible in everything she wrote. It is a southern voice, a Georgian voice, the voice of a writer who, returned home for good, seems determined to shuck off the sophistication she had picked up in the north. Significantly, Marion Montgomery called the relevant volume of his critical trilogy *Why Flannery O'Connor Stayed Home*.

If she was a Catholic author, if her writing was influenced by her faith, O'Connor almost never chose Catholic subjects for her stories. Her characters are the underclass of the South, most of them haunted by a fundamentalist, Bible-thumping, evangelical Christianity. Her ability imaginatively to occupy the outlook of men and women and children almost retarded in their simplicity is equaled only by Steinbeck in *Of Mice and Men*. Her approach to her characters is anything but condescending. In them she sees the mystery and dignity of the human person.

All art, she maintained, is anagogic. That is, all fiction which is more than mere diversion conveys the awesome battle between good and evil that is fought out in every human soul. But how is the Catholic writer to convey to a secular audience this sense of the importance of the person and his actions? The Catholic writer, she felt, should not take the Church or Catholic things as subject, that made the task too easy, and it also limited the audience.

She could kid Tom Stritch, professor at Notre Dame, about the dangers of being converted to culture; she affected a backwoodsy manner, but her letters contain references to a wide variety of Catholic writers: Claude Tresmontant, Romano Gaurdini, Fulton Sheen, Frank Sheed, Sigrid Undset, Edwin O'Connor, Charles Peguy, J. F. Powers, Caroline Gordon, Graham Greene, Walker Percy, François Mauriac, Thomas Merton, Baron von Huegel, Teilhard de Chardin, Joseph Conrad, Henri Daniel-Rops, Paul Claudel, etc., etc. The girl from Milledgeville, Georgia not only practiced her faith but lived in an imaginative and intellectual Catholic ambience.

She regarded her writing as a vocation and her reflections on it are instructive for any aspiring Catholic writer. The essays collected in *Mystery and Manners* and the letters brought together by Sally Fitzgerald in the large volume called *The Habit of Being* provide an instructive contrast with the voice we hear in the fiction. The authors listed above are cited off-handedly, almost as if she did not wish to draw attention to the scope of her reading. It is clear that she was drawn to authors who accepted as true the Christian vision of human life. But of course it was not abstractions that could be helpful to her in her fiction.

A writer needs a voice and a place – she thought all good writing is regional writing – people and events that can carry a message she would never state explicitly in her fiction. Her material was the rural South, and this meant that her characters are for the most part Protestants. In their exaggerated religiosity they enable her to portray the drama of salvation as it goes on in every soul.

In one of her letters she speaks of a preacher who had chained a lamb to a cross and sacrificed it in front of his congregation. Grotesque? Showmanship? Maybe. But she thought it might have been as close as he could come to the Mass. It is that ability to grasp the latent significance in the grotesque that marks the writing of Flannery O'Connor.

Readers, among them her mother, complained because she wrote about such odd and grotesque characters. Her response is one only a deeply religious writer could have made. "We are all grotesque."

FRANK O'MALLEY

A whole Catholic world was opened to his students, not as lore, not as something to chatter about, but as addressing the deep and persistent questions to which every life is an answer.

In those days there was a lounge in the tower of O'Shaughnessy Hall to which the faculty repaired for that wrangling gossip that has always provided the ambience of academe. Coffee and rolls were available in the morning, and that is where I would see him. Impeccably dressed, always standing, in one hand were his class notes, in the other, slightly shaking, his cup of coffee. Frank O'Malley, teacher, already a Notre Dame legend when I joined the faculty. I find it hard to believe that he was not yet fifty, actually forty-six. He seemed affably aloof, but it was really shyness. I don't think I would have been surprised to be told he was destined to become a symbol transcending the South Bend campus. A symbol of many things.

Of the vitality of the pre-conciliar Church.

Of the primacy of teaching over research.

Of Catholic literature as a unique fusion of the temporal and eternal.

He was born in 1909 and came to Notre Dame in 1928 and that is where he stayed, living on campus until his death in May 1974, on the eve of retirement. His Master's dissertation was on Archbishop Lamy of Sante Fe in relation to Willa Cather's novel. He never took a doctorate. He became a teacher, and his subject was literature, particularly Catholic literature.

It is, alas, largely forgotten how lively were the 1930s and '40s and '50s in the American Church. There was talk of the Catholic cultural renaissance, already under way in Europe and come to us via Jacques Maritain, Chesterton, Yves Simon, and Waldemar Gurian. Gurian, along with O'Malley, founded *The Review of Politics*, and it is in the Review that much of the meager output of O'Malley can be found. His vision of Catholic culture was one in which faith and reason, mind and imagination, thought and life, formed a single whole. Religious knowledge, he insisted, is the highest kind of knowledge. And literature is as much an expression of it as philosophy and theology.

Such knowledge is a corrective of the status quo. O'Malley was the kind of Catholic who did not long for entry into the secular world; he wanted that world transformed. A Catholic education was an opportunity to acquire the culture necessary to redeem the time. He introduced generations of Notre Dame students to Christopher Dawson, Etienne Gilson, Henri de Lubac, Vladimir Soloviev, Robert Hugh Benson, Peter Wust, Berdyaev, Romano Guardini, Josef Pieper, along with Blake, Milton, T. S. Eliot, and, surprisingly, D. H. Lawrence. Catholic novelists like Waugh, Mauriac, Greene, Bloy, Bernanos, Peguy, and Sigrid Undset were part of his repertoire. He loved Gerard Manly Hopkins, and his own poetry is imitative, not very successfully, of the Jesuit poet. Newman, Aquinas, Maritain, Claudel – a whole Catholic world was opened to his students, not as lore, not as something to chatter about, but as addressing the deep and persistent questions to which every life is an answer.

O'Malley was unclubbable, both locally and beyond the campus. One is almost surprised to learn that he attended a meeting of the Renascence Society. Maritain introduced Frank to the University of Chicago, to Hutchins and Adler, and to the Committee on Social Thought. He was a correspondent of Hugh Taylor who nearly convinced O'Malley to come to Princeton and get his doctorate. He stayed where he was.

O'Malley figures in most Notre Dame memoirs, those of Ed Fischer, Tom Stritch, Father Hesburgh, and in 1992 a symposium on him was part of the sesquicentennial celebration of the founding of the university. But O'Malley had not liked the way Notre Dame was moving in his lifetime. Not long ago a sign went up at the university entrances. Notre Dame, A National Catholic Research University. O'Malley would have wept. As he would have wept at the voiding of the classrooms of the eager, cultivated, and celebratory approach toward Catholicism that characterized his own teaching.

He had a recurrent dream, aided and abetted by former students, of a new institution, Christ College. John Meaney's *O'Malley of Notre Dame* gives an extended account of it. There was a California possibility, another in Ohio, but it remained only a dream. The thought of Frank O'Malley leaving Notre Dame was more than O'Malley himself could bear. The wider scene provided the contrast for his dream college.

> [It would differ] especially from the educational establishments of this day, structures without souls, drained of the vital sap of fundamental intuitions and, in the suppression of all determinate differences of intellectual position or at least of the actual relevance of such differences, rendered purposeless, meaningless, occasions at best of a certain dubious social conditioning.

How ironic that it is such soul-less institutions, grown worse, that Catholic universities now seek to imitate.

Like most great teachers, O'Malley was not an original thinker. He was a retailer of the ideas and images and metaphors of others. His writings echo with Maritain and Dawson and Pieper and all the authors he loved and made his students love. Tom Stritch has pointed out that, while O'Malley loved wit and humor, these were not traits of his.

His teaching was protreptic, aimed not merely at mastery of a subject, but at stirring the soul to a sense of its ultimate vocation. Stritch called him a prophet. He was certainly trying to get young people to see the awesome possibilities in themselves, chiefly the possibility of sanctity.

I would call him a dinosaur, but dinosaurs are popular now. O'Malley's was a singular voice in his own time. He would seem completely alien now to careerist Catholic academics and administrators willing to deal away almost anything for a little recognition from the human soul's natural enemies. But what he celebrated remains, those poets and philosophers and novelists whose work, like his, was permeated with the faith. They were all in their way pilgrims of the absolute.

Here are a few lines from Ernest Sandeen's valedictory poem to Frank O'Malley.

> You christened writers of indiscreetly
> visionary words, the baptized
> and unbaptized alike, while awed
> multitudes of the young looked on.
>
> You gospelled four decades of rich and poor men's
> sons showing them where the soul is.
> And each day you knotted them thongs to whip
> the money-changers from the temple door.

Frank had his flaws. He drank too much. And he was a Democrat, for all his iconoclasm a partisan who at least during elections seemed to think politics matters. He lies now in the community cemetery at Notre Dame but on the campus his memory has thinned, as wispy as the smoke from his interminable cigarette. He lives on in his students, whose tributes to him bring a catch to the throat. Let Ernie Sandeen speak our farewell.

> But we salute you now as then
> with love, across no greater distance
> than you always kept, immaculate
> and warm, between yourself and us.

CHARLES PEGUY

When he sat off on foot for Chartres, he was a man who probably thought of himself as an all around failure.

In 1912, a spare man with a spade beard set off on foot from Paris, his destination the cathedral of Chartres. His name was Charles Peguy, he was just shy of forty years of age, he was a poet, pamphleteer, patriot and, above all, a Catholic who cherished his faith the more because of the years he had spent away from it. Two years later he would be one of the first to fall for France in World War I. Eighty years later he is mentioned often, written of some, read little. Who was Charles Peguy?

Many first encountered him in Raïssa Maritain's memoirs. He enters the Maritains' life as owner of a bookstore, *Cahiers de la Quinzaine*, which can still be seen on the Rue de la Sorbonne, a vestigial rebuke to the institution across the street. Raïssa presents us with the portrait of a slightly older man – married, with children he had not had baptized, a socialist, a man of enormous integrity who had broken with his former political allies, living a precarious life.

In her second book of memoirs, *Adventures in Grace*, Raïssa discusses Peguy's religious difficulties. Her account begins with a quotation from Peguy, "I have found the Faith again, I am a Catholic." Thus he came before the American Catholic reader as a writer who, having wandered in the byways of socialism and uneasy agnosticism, returned to the faith and found in Joan of Arc the overwhelming symbol of France.

The fact is that he wrote *Jeanne d'Arc* almost a decade before his return to the Church in 1907, and it is tempting to think that she attracted him because of her failure, her martyrdom, her victory in defeat. Peguy's own life did not describe a rising line. It was not exactly a spiral downward either, but a looping progression from hope through half-accomplishment to reversal. When he sat off on foot for Chartres, he was a man who probably thought of himself as an all-around failure.

With writers, it is customary to trade off a dissatisfying life for the stories or poems that come out of it, counting the sacrifice of the poet small price to pay for his poetry. This romantic conception of the artist dies hard. In any case, Peguy would have repudiated it with disdain. He wanted recognition and acclaim. He felt he deserved it. He did not receive it. Is there success in failure?

The Christian signs upon himself the cross which symbolizes the cruel execution of his publicly discredited Lord. *In hoc signo vinces?* But victory under this sign almost always looks like worldly defeat. One of the fascinations of Peguy is that he sought worldly acclaim by writing on themes which call into question worldly acclaim.

> Only you know our loveliest sentiments
> Last no more than the space of a day
> And the strongest and most lasting love
> Lasts no more than moments.

Those lines are from *Eve*, said to be the longest poem in French, one thousand, nine hundred quatrains, or seven thousand six hundred forty-four lines. That is the size of a good-sized novel. A pretty hefty bid for attention.

His prose writings are studded with *mots*. "There are lots of honest men. You can tell them by the way they do bad things badly." "Experts on youth are almost as sad as experts on love." "Kantianism has pure hands, but it has no hands." "One is no longer a poet after twelve years of age." "One word is always better than many." And, fair warning perhaps, "One should never believe what a poet says."

The Maritains, in their fervor as converts, confided in Peguy what had happened to them. "But I too have come to that," he cried. What did the poet mean? Jacques was not edified to learn that Peguy missed Mass on Sunday as well as Ascension Day. What kind of faith was this that did not express itself in the practices the faith required? But Peguy's marriage was not blessed and his children were unbaptized and his wife was opposed to rectifying either. They had married in a civil cere- mony, she came of revolutionary stock, and Peguy appears to have felt bound by the nature of the compact they had entered into, considering it a matter of justice. To go to Mass would be to endure the suffering of separating himself from his family, and to be unable to receive communion. This was Peguy's agonizing situation. He may serve as a kind of patron for those caught in similar seemingly insoluble circumstances.

Jacques Maritain made a disastrous visit to Peguy's wife to convince her that, since baptism was a meaningless gesture in her eyes, she should accede to Peguy's desires. The visit descended into theological wrangling. Raïssa tries to put the best face on it, but it is difficult not to see the visit as enormously imprudent. It caused a rift between the Maritains and Peguy.

Peguy had been a champion of Dreyfus, and fell out with his former allies. He was a difficult friend and a ferocious foe. He returned to the faith but not to communion, and it was only on the battlefield that he reentered the sacramental life. Peguy is a puzzle, no doubt about it. His poetry, which translates with diffi- culty, has come into English, but his prose has not. The fifteen years of his *Cahiers*, chock full of his great polemics and crusades, are exciting to read. His blast against Durkheim and sociology makes telling points. His feeling that the Church, by treating the apostate Ernest Renan with such gentleness, seemed to have adopted the liberalism that had led Renan out of the priesthood and out of the Church, is a shrewd analysis.

There are French writers who have written out of a Catholic sensibility but whose lives have been far from edifying. One thinks of Chateaubriand and Barbey d'Aureyville, to keep exam- ples discreetly in the past. Peguy does not fall into this category.

Far from it. With the return of faith came a settled Catholic out-look, that pervaded his life and everything he wrote. "It is probable that he did not have that 'illumination' which suddenly seized Claudel one Christmas afternoon at Notre Dame during the singing of the Magnificat, but that for him an interior change took place by slow increments. When he made his remark to Lotte [that he had regained the faith], he was sure of himself, and when he declared himself subject to the absolute 'order' of Our Lady of Chartres he had accepted the faith as a gift." (Louis Perche)

In 1910 appeared *The Mystery of the Charity of Joan of Arc.* The adoption of an openly Catholic outlook alienated many subscribers to the *Cahiers*, who had come aboard when Peguy was a socialist. He gained new readers, of course, some of them as equivocal as those he had lost. He was embraced as an unques-tioning patriot, a hero of the right. But Peguy's politics seem as non-ideological as those of Bernanos.

Peguy deserves a revival of interest on the part of Catholics. Anyone can love the poetry, but the prose, should it find its way into English, would claim, I think, a wide readership. Passionate, provoking, in the world but not of it, living his life in a kind of limbo, Peguy ended as a hero, both moral and military. Joan of Arc must have welcomed him home.

WALKER PERCY

The secular reader, moving on a superficial level, could take Percy to be illustrating what the secular reader assumes Christian belief to be. Certifiable madness. But what is a scandal and a folly to the worldly, is the only sanity there is.

He was the non-Catholic's favorite Catholic novelist, and that was worrisome. Secular readers obviously relish tales of how awful it is to be Catholic, how repressive to be told that guilt follows on sin, when of course we all now know that you're okay and I'm okay and guilt is just an unwillingness to get in touch with oneself.

Write a novel with mad priests, sadistic nuns, and parents who teach you that sexuality is not a team sport, thereby thwarting your cheerful natural impulse to mate with everyone in sight, and with impunity, and you may make it as a Catholic novelist in the late 20th-century in the U.S.A.

Did Walker Percy sell out? Did he cater to the anti-Catholicism that is the anti-Semitism of the liberal?

Trained as a medical doctor, converted to Catholicism, one of the most laid-back of writers, yet remarkably productive, Walker Percy began his literary career with an amazing novel, *The Moviegoer* (1962) which won the National Book Award, and followed it with *The Last Gentleman* (1966). Then, in *Love in the Ruins* (1971), he altered from being the latest in the amazing list of Southern writers and became what would have been *sui generis* if it weren't for Flannery O'Connor and a couple of others – a Southern Catholic writer.

The evolution, or more properly the gradual revelation, was a logical one, since what Percy was making clear was the ultimate foundation of his meditative criticism of man in the modern world. It had been possible to see this, as the title of his second novel suggested, as an appalled gentleman's reaction to the ascendancy of the Snopeses in contemporary America. But this was not the lament of a nostalgic Confederate who wanted to think of the War Between the States as one between Northern vulgarity and the Southern championship of the good life.

Love in the Ruins may be Walker Percy's best novel. A sign that he himself thought so is the fact that his last novel, *The Thanatos Syndrome* (1987), was a sequel to it. Here is its beginning. "Now in these dread latter days of the old violent beloved U.S.A. and of the Christ-forgetting Christ-haunted death-dealing Western world I came to myself in a grove of young pines and the question came to me: has it happened at last?" *It* is the end of the world, the beginning of the end, end times. Percy had entered his apocalyptic phase.

Six years later in 1977, *Lancelot* appeared, with lines from Dante set before the story.

> He sank so low that all means
> for his salvation were gone,
> except showing him the lost people.
> For this I visited the region of the dead . . .

The movies are back, but this time it is the making of one, not the passive absorption of them in a dark theater.

The Second Coming (1980) made clear the technique Percy had evolved to make his increasingly overt Catholic sensibility palatable to a wide range of readers. The hero escapes from a mental institution, descends into a cave in search of a proof for the existence of God and a sign of the apocalypse. Are we to think of those Christ haunted crazies of Flannery O'Connor's, whom she saw as what happens when Christianity becomes unmoored from the Church? Not quite.

Percy had come to see that seriously to believe the Christian message nowadays is to qualify as insane. The trick then is to accept this judgment and to show from the vantage point of this putative insanity the genuine insanity of the standpoint from which the Christian is seen as crazy. Oblique. Indirect. Kierkegaardian. Artful.

The secular reader, moving on a superficial level, could take Percy to be illustrating what the secular reader assumes Christian belief to be. Certifiable madness. But what is a scandal and a folly to the worldly, is the only sanity there is. *The Thanatos Syndrome* happened to be Walker Percy's last book. It appeared in 1987, and he died in 1990. Perhaps he would have written another novel, but it is difficult to imagine where he could have gone – and taken the secular reader with him.

The last novel picks up and extends Percy's concern with the tendency to regard human beings as things to be altered, manipulated, and controlled by drugs and oppressive psychological techniques. In danger of being lost is the free and responsible agent, wounded by sin, capable of salvation, who is the concern of Christ's salvific act. A recognition of the human capacity for evil, as a consequence of freedom, is a presupposition of salvation.

"For some time now I have noticed that something strange is occurring in our region. I have noticed it both in the patients I have treated and in ordinary encounters with people. At first they were only suspicions. But yesterday my suspicions were confirmed. I was called to the hospital for a consultation and there was an opportunity to make an examination."

The novel is set in Walker Percy's neighborhood. He has no need for travel to find an objective correlative for his spiritual concern. The priest who eventually passes judgment on what is happening is mad, crazy, dismissable on naturalistic grounds. Percy exhibits an almost Dostoevskian penchant for the holy madman as spokesman.

In his three prose collections, Walker Percy ranges from wildly comic exercises to sober essays, to apocalyptic effusions which rival those of any of his fictional characters. *The Message in the Bottle* (1975) is a well organized book on the subject of language. An analytic philosopher who reviewed it undertook to chide one of the masters of English usage on the nature of language. He might have been invented by Percy.

Lost in the Cosmos (1983), "The Last Self-Help Book," is wildly funny, employing what became a favorite genre for Percy, the self-administered questionnaire. I would say that no one can read it without finding himself eased into the kind of self-examination urged on us by spiritual writers – but what then is to be made of the wide secular readership the book had?

A sign that he had gone too far may be found in the resounding silence that greeted the posthumously published non-fiction book (his third), *Sign-Posts in a Strange Land*, edited by Patrick Samway (1991). The final collection bears similarities to both of the earlier ones since Father Samway, to his credit, is reluctant to let anything go uncollected.

The death of Walker Percy does not simply leave a gap in the ranks of Catholic novelists. In many respects, he was, if not the last gentleman, certainly the last Catholic novelist of consequence in this country. Now we have whimpering whining pseudo-confessional schlock from disenchanted Catholics whose aim is currying favor with their pagan contemporaries. What Walker Percy would have thought of them can be guessed from his mock Donahue show in *Lost in the Cosmos*.

JOSEF PIEPER

Josef Pieper is a Thomist who has thought through what Thomas wrote and passed on what he has understood and extended the same approach into areas Thomas never dreamt of.

The old joke about the writer who did not have enough time to write a short letter has its academic counterpart in the teacher who knows so much he can no longer make himself understood. One of the benefits of the American university system is that few scholars are permitted to teach only graduate students. They must also face undergraduates, and this is the true test of their knowledge. Can they meet the tyro on his own ground and lead him into a subject that looms as a vast *terra incognita*?

Research takes one far from the starting points of a discipline, and it can require an imaginative feat to occupy once again the shoes of the beginner. An inability – I do not say unwillingness – to do this renders suspect the status of arcane accomplishments.

This by way of fanfare to a paean of praise for one of the most intelligible of philosophers, Josef Pieper, who died in 1997 at the age of 94. Pieper first came to the attention of American readers when T. S. Eliot wrote the preface to the English translation of *Leisure, the Basis of Culture*. If this had been a solitary achievement it would still impress, but that extraordinary work is only one of dozens of such short books Pieper has written over the course of his extended active career, most of it spent at the University of Münster.

To observe that Pieper is a Thomist can occasion surprise among those who think of contemporary students of Aquinas as speaking in Latinate jargon about topics of interest only to those with an acquired taste for them. A reader expecting extended exegesis of texts of Thomas, or even constant allusions to the Master, may be disappointed – or perhaps pleasantly surprised by a prose which directly addresses the reader in a familiar language on matters of compelling interest.

Of course the whole point of the Thomistic Revival was to bring the thought of Thomas to bear on a contemporary situation very much in need of its light. Responses to this desire of every Pope since Leo XIII (except perhaps John Paul I), have been various. The Leonine Commission, set up to prepare a reliable text, is still fussing away after more than a century. Its editions are swamped in erudition and now lean toward bizarre orthography. Perhaps the Commission should have set up a two-track operation, one devoted to Leo's charge, the other to the paleographical pleasantries in which experts delight, but which seldom contribute to or enhance an intelligent reading of Thomas.

There have been many who have sought to develop the relevance of Thomas for issues of our time, and there have been some who addressed the general reading public. But no one has done either as effectively and habitually as Josef Pieper.

A few years ago, I visited him in Münster, renewing an acquaintance that had begun when he took part in a Perspectives Series on ethics I arranged at Notre Dame. His study was filled with the work of his artist wife; he was then in his late eighties and still at work. It occurred to me that he himself did not fully realize the dimensions of his philosophical achievement. Ever since I have been asking myself how best to describe what Pieper has done.

In the first instance, he has provided a keen pleasure to his reader, the aesthetic pleasure of a well-made book, and the logical pleasure of discourse that moves from the familiar to the unfamiliar. But that is such an abstract way of putting it.

Take a book like *The End of Time*, a meditation on the philosophy of history whose motto is drawn from Hamann. "Who can hope to obtain proper concepts of the present, without knowing the future?" But what can philosophers know of the future? The little they discern must be supplemented. The book culminates in a discussion of the Anti-Christ.

Take *Happiness and Contemplation*, perhaps more typical. Here Pieper undertakes to explain and defend the view that our happiness will be found only in contemplation, a notion he takes from Aristotle and Thomas Aquinas, but which is discussed not as a scholarly or historical matter, but as the only adequate answer to the human quest.

The professional scholar, the accomplished Thomist, reads Pieper with amazement. It is not simply that Pieper can popularize the technical and difficult; one finds in his little books fundamental contributions to ongoing learned disputes. No one has written more wisely on the relation between thinking and doing than Pieper, yet there are no obstacles of erudition between the reader and the presentation.

How does he do it? All philosophers long to be intelligible, yet become accustomed to the glazed eyes of listeners when they try to convey what it is they are working on. Suddenly it seems so remote and irrelevant to ordinary life. Yet here is Pieper, making those difficult things intelligible without in any way trivializing them.

C. S. Lewis had a similar knack but his works do not have the range Pieper's do. Of course Pieper was blessed with an exceptionally long life, with a clarity of mind which never deserted him. There is an old adage that he himself cites. *Primum vivere, deinde philosophari*. Philosophize only on the basis of lived experience. The complement to that is the requirement that philosophy retain its relevance to life. It does this only when its practitioner achieves the goal of the whole effort, wisdom.

That, I think, is the mark of Josef Pieper's achievement. In reading him, we are listening to a wise man. Some are Thomists in the manner of fans; others are Thomists in the manner of painstaking readers of the texts of Thomas. Josef Pieper was a

Thomist who has thought through what Thomas wrote and passed on what he has understood and extended the same approach into areas Thomas never dreamt of.

In introducing him to English readers, T. S. Eliot contrasted Pieper with the then dominant mode of philosophizing, Logical Positivism, which Eliot characterized as "a method of philosophizing without insight and wisdom." From the outset, it was the sapiential tone of Pieper's thought that struck the reader. Philosophy is of course the pursuit and love of wisdom. But what is wisdom? What men can know of God. Eliot noted that Pieper's "mind is submissive to what he believes to be the great, the main tradition of European thought; his originality is subdued and unostentatious." One might perhaps add that originality is a bonus rather than the aim of his thinking.

Among the heavy debts we owe to Father Joseph Fessio and his Ignatius Press is the reissue of many Pieper titles and the first English edition of many more. These appear in delightful and impeccable typography. Many more titles – some reprinted, some new translations – are now being issued by St. Augustine's Press, with the intention that soon his entire *oeuvre* will be available to the English-speaking world. It is only fitting that Josef Pieper should be within such easy reach of the readers for whom he writes.

J. F. POWERS
The Principality of Powers

Who has not wondered how the priests depicted by Powers, with their relatively minor flaws, could have given way in so short a time to the scandal-ridden clergy of the 1990s?

When *The Prince of Darkness*, J. F. Powers's first collection of short stories, appeared, it was assumed that many of his characters were closely modeled on clerics of the Archdiocese of St. Paul. It was even whispered that he had a clerical informant without whom, it was apparently assumed, he could not have written so tellingly of priests and bishops and nuns and rectories and all the associated lore. Sometimes such a misconception is the sincerest form of praise.

Powers, a native of Illinois, has spent most of his life in Minnesota, at or in the vicinity of St. John's University, a Benedictine foundation. The chief thing about him as a writer is that he writes. He communicates with the wider public through his stories, and in no other way. His stories are Catholic to the core, with priests the preferred subject.

But fiction is more manners than substance and undeniably the midwestern priests that populate Powers's stories are no more. A great deal has happened to the Church since Powers began to write and, wisely I think, he has decided not to adjust his imaginative vision to the changing flux but to continue to find in the pre-conciliar priest his proper subject. In *Wheat That Springeth Green* (1988), Powers did attempt a story of the Church after Vatican II, but the strength of the novel derives from the same inspiration as his earlier fiction. Despite the dates, the priests are pre-Vatican II – and I mean that as praise.

The midwestern rectory, the mildly abrasive relations between pastor and assistant, between the priest and his enigmatic bishop, the continuing threat of the housekeeper, the go-getter priest who wants to put his parish or order on the map – this is Powers's world. His genius is to tease the essence of human conflict out of quibbles over forks and typing tables and parish cats. His stories are delightful in many ways, but one of the ways could hardly have been foreseen by the author.

In *Dubliners*, James Joyce caught his characters at a moment meant to reveal the vacuousness of their lives. But is that why the John Ford movie based on "The Dead" attracts us? The Dublin Joyce fled has become an object of nostalgia. Powers sees men whose awesome priestly function has degenerated into routine, a job. Nowadays their temptations almost endear them to us rather than shock us. They are somewhere between the saccharine celluloid priests of *The Bells of St. Mary's* and the prairie priest in F. Scott Fitzgerald's dark story, "Absolution," with which he considered opening *The Great Gatsby* (which would have made clear that the hero was a Catholic).

Powers is chiefly a short story writer – his two novels have the air of collections – and he is not prolific, having published only five volumes during a career half a century old. The title story of his first collection, *Prince of Darkness*, introduced a priest who would be a recurrent character, Ernest Burner. (Sometimes seen through the eyes of the rectory cat.) His hobby of photography necessitates a dark room and that is the origin of his (old) nickname. Burner is still an assistant although all his classmates now have their own parishes. He golfs, he takes flying lessons, he orders a beer with his burger at a drive-in. His basic fault is portrayed as gluttony, but Evelyn Waugh was right to see that it is the capital sin of sloth that dogs the steps of Powers's priests.

Sloth is weariness with and distaste for the sacred. The priest who does not pursue sanctity will lead an empty and seemingly trivial life, or so the saints assure us. Reading his office, administering the sacraments, saying Mass, can become mere functions he performs. His plight will be manifested in idiosyncrasy, pettiness, the need for distraction. What the present-day reader may find hard to find in these stories is a sense of evil. Imperfection, venial sin, yes, but mortal sin? The only instance of the latter is the drunkenness of Father Desmond, but he is overwhelmed by a sense of his unworthiness to be a priest. Most Catholics nowadays would give a lot to have the rectories of the nation populated with Powers's priests.

Nonetheless Powers may provide a clue to what has gone wrong with the American priesthood. That comfortable life – mindful of privilege and perks (the clergy pass on the railroad, for example), used to deference from the laity – while hardly riddled with vice, can be seen as the counterpart of the life led by Graham Greene's Mexican priest before the persecution began. Some Mexican priests apostasized; many were martyred. Greene's priest is being pursued – by the faithful who need him as much as by the *jefe* who would kill him – and he ruefully contrasts his fugitive life with the pleasant one he led before the revolution.

Who has not wondered how the priests depicted by Powers, with their relatively minor flaws, could have given way in so short a time to the scandal-ridden clergy of the 1990s? The hero of Powers's first novel, *Morte D'Urban* (winner of the National Book Award when that was still a real distinction), comes all right in the end, but in a world of pederasts, dissidents, and malcontents, he looks pretty good to us even before he is beaned by the golf ball that wakes him up. What explanation of this change can Powers provide?

Fairly or not, the image of the Catholic priest in the United States today is of a man unsure of his role, fearful to preach Church doctrine on sexual matters, allegedly chafing under the burden of celibacy, and in a few tragic cases engaged in seriously sinful behavior. The priests of J. F. Powers have their defects but the reader is struck by the clarity they have as to what they are and what they ought to be. Their problem is one of performance, not theology.

By contrast, the young men coming into the priesthood today have not received the kind of training that once was the rule. Rigorous seminary discipline did not guarantee sanctity of course, but its absence has results that are all too predictable. Not even Powers could have imagined a clergy talking the lingo of pop psychology and bishops speaking of pederasts as in need of counseling.

> How did we get from there to here? Sloth is one of the capital sins.

PRINCIPALITIES AND POWERS

"Phil was weak. Monsignor Renton was strong, and Father Urban, though strong, had no desire to come between old friends. Hence his sometimes halting speech, his turning of the other cheek. 'Your ass is out, Father' – 'And yet, Monsignor.'"

Will Monsignor Renton build the larger church his growing parish needs or stick with the old one because of its sentimental meaning for him? Father Urban is the protagonist of *Morte D'Urban*, J. F. Powers 1963 novel, winner of the National Book Award. It marked the apex of a writing career that found its inspiration in the Catholic clergy of the Midwest. He published another collection of short stories, *Look How the Fish Live* (1975) and a novel, *Wheat That Springeth Green* (1988) but Vatican II killed off his subject. He died in 1999 in elective obscurity, at home on the campus of a Benedictine monastery in Minnesota.

A native of Illinois, who lived most of his life in or near St. Cloud, Minnesota – with extended stays in Ireland – Powers was a layman who found his subject in the "submerged population" (as Frank O'Connor put it), of the pre-conciliar Catholic clergy of the Midwest. In an era when stories about priests in Catholic magazines were piously saccharine, Powers published his wonderfully funny and realistic stories in *The New Yorker*. He was never ignored, always admired, but ever aloof from the literary scene. No one could have imagined him schmoozing editors or other writers at a Manhattan cocktail party. Some years ago, given an award by the Wethersfield Institute, he was cajoled into leaving his Minnesota redoubt, no easy matter, but once in New York he welcomed the opportunity to visit a few jazz clubs. (Jazz musicians afforded him a rare alternative subject to priests.) One night, looking up Fifth Avenue toward the Park, he wondered what it cost to live in one of those posh apartments, as his friend Garrison Keillor did at the time. Jon Hassler, another Minnesota author, was also a friend and Powers's wife Betty Wahl was a writer too. My best guess was, "Plenty." He thought for a moment. "Think of how much you'd have to write to afford that."

For a writer who lived by his pen but was not prolific, rural Minnesota was a wiser place to settle. And then his basic subject, the clergy of the Midwest, was there. He published only two novels and three collections of short stories. His second novel was published in 1988, a quarter century after his first, and he said ruefully that his editor had not been alive when he published the first. Both novels seem to be collections of short stories, the genre in which Powers excelled.

Although Powers wrote mainly of the diocesan clergy, he founded two fictional orders, the Clementines and the Dolomites. In either case, there is an ironic contrast between the priest as *alter Christus* and as a man trying to make his way in an organization described as second only to Standard Oil in its efficiency. Powers's cites this contrast with tongue in cheek. Bishops act with whimsical power. Father Burner, of "The Prince of Darkness," a perennial assistant, longs for a parish of his own, has a crucial interview with his bishop and is given his new assignment in a sealed envelope which he is told not to open until after Mass the next morning. In his car he tears it open. "You will report on August 8 to the Reverend Michael Furlong, to begin your duties that day as his assistant. I trust that in your new appointment you will find not peace but a sword."

Powers's bishops, pastors, and superiors are all like Father Burner's ordinary. Their underlings measure out their lives with

coffee spoons. The dreaded nightly card game with a domineering housekeeper, clerical passes on trains, petty struggles. One
pastor won't give his assistant a key to the rectory, another
inspects his car after each use by his assistant. Unlike Bernanos's
priests, those in Powers's stories do not seem to be in tortured
quest of sanctity. They want the little perks of their world. The
best analogy to them, perhaps, is found in Trollope's Barsetshire.
Like Trollope, Powers never condescends to his characters. It has
been said that J. D. Salinger loved his characters more than God
does. Powers loved his almost as much as God does, because he
had no illusions about them.

Someone reading Powers today might think that these are pre-
Vatican II horror stories, a portrait of an authoritative Church
from which priests, and laity, have been liberated. This would be
a fundamental misreading. It is true that Powers lost his subject
because of the changes that followed the Council, but it is safe to
guess that he would have found today's priests an even richer
source of comedy. His second novel fails because it tries to place
priests of the forties and fifties in a post-conciliar world. He never
got the hang of the last quarter of the 20th century. But he is
unsurpassed on the pre-conciliar clergy.

Priests fascinate lay people just because there is a sacramental
significance to them. Their office requires a deeper living of the
Christian life, and yet they are vessels of clay. For the believer they
can provide a privileged instance of the way the world encroaches
on the soul. By taking trivial events, Powers is able to underscore
that most lives, including priestly lives, are caught up in quotidian,
petty events, yet this is the arena in which one will save or lose his
soul. That is the subtext of every Powers's story. He is a Catholic
writer in the way Dante was. The stakes are eternal, but they are
decided in the moment, by seemingly disproportional acts. Paolo
and Francesca are damned by an adulterous kiss. Powers's priests
can go to hell for picking on an assistant. That is why they retain
their interest even in a time when the devil and hell and the capital sins are seldom mentioned.

PIERS PAUL READ

The Third Day is the most overt theological drama Read has written thus far. His Catholicism has been visible from the beginning.

Most readers will recognize the title *Alive!* and others will have seen the movie made of the book, but few, I wager, will know the author's name. I do not say, remember it. Authors learn how anonymous they remain to most readers. And that is just as well, of course – it is what is written, not who writes it, that should captivate us.

The author of *Alive!* is Piers Paul Read.

Doubtless he has grown used to being identified in this way. But *Alive!* is a non-fiction book, and Piers Paul Read is a novelist. It is because he is a Catholic novelist that he could write so powerful and empathetic a book about those survivors of a plane crash in the Andes. He has written another non-fiction book about Chernobyl. I am sure it is an excellent book. But it is to his novels that we should go.

His *oeuvre* is odd, which means that he follows his own line, choosing not to repeat himself. One is struck by how different his books are from one another. An early novel, *Monk Dawson*, conveys the school experience of Catholics in England. A later novel, *The Professor's Daughter*, is set in the United States and attempts to convey the chaotic campus during the days when protesting the Vietnam War seemed to be the major academic preoccupation.

Read has written historical novels, *romans fleuves*; he has tried to occupy the skin of characters from places and cultures very different from his own. *A Married Man* (1979) is billed as a novel of love, marriage, and adultery, usually a promissory claim on a paperback cover. Long before one gets to the end, one knows he is far from the land of schlock.

> "I find it strange," said John, "that you make vows when you marry to last until you are separated by death, and yet now that Clare is dead I feel no less married to her than I did before."
>
> "Perhaps marriages are made in heaven after all," said Eustace.
>
> "And yet Christ said, didn't He, that there are no husbands and wives in Heaven?"
>
> "We can't expect to understand it all," said Eustace, shaking his head. "We have to take what we can get and make the most of it."
>
> "And hope," said John, "that He whose understanding matters will understand."

Not the denouement the cover would have prepared you for.

A Season in the West (1988) tells of a Czech writer who comes to England and meets his translator. Coming from an oppressive, Communist culture, he expects more from the culture of the free world than, alas, it has to offer. Read is able to appraise his own culture through the perceptive appraising eyes of Josef Birek.

The Free Frenchman (1986), a very large novel, tells the story of France from 1914 to 1950. The perceptive reader will detect that the author is a Roman Catholic. Often this is not simply a background assumption, but becomes thematic. Nowhere is this more the case than in *The Third Day* (1992), perhaps Read's most successful novel.

The premise of the novel is the discovery by an Israeli archeologist who comes upon a burial urn beneath the Dome of the Rock. The urn contains the body of a crucified male of the first century. On the skull are marks that could have been made by a crown of thorns. The novel is every bit as intriguing as this beginning. Read is able to explore the assumptions of some recent theology and biblical scholarship. A casualty of the apparent find is a priest who, in despair that he has dedicated his life to a myth, loses his faith, leaves the priesthood, spins out of control. His is a more honest reaction to the seeming disproof of the Resurrection than that of a cardinal who embarks on damage control and, in a vein that is unfortunately not unfamiliar, argues that belief in the Resurrection is perfectly compatible with the discovery of the remains of Jesus.

The Third Day is the most overt theological drama Read has written thus far. His Catholicism has been visible from the beginning. Born in 1941, Read was brought up in Yorkshire and educated at Cambridge. He has lived out of England from time to time and has traveled widely. Married, he has four children. How does he, as a husband and father, regard the current confusion in the Church?

In 1991, Piers Paul Read contributed a pamphlet to the Claridge *Blasts* series entitled *Quo Vadis?* An earlier entry in the series had been A. N. Wilson's anti-Catholic screed. Read's contribution is a gifted Catholic layman's look at the Catholic Church in England. He recalls the tumultuous wake of Vatican II, with particular emphasis on the effect of the sexual revolution on moral theology, the devastating impact of radical feminism, the confusions of liberation theology, and the notion of an alternative magisterium of theologians. *Quo Vadis?* is a fresh look at a familiar picture, but one that has not lost its power to astonish and dismay. Read is particularly good on the confusion in catechetics, and his protest is that of a parent whose children have been subjected to the nonsense he narrates.

Read wrote while the *Catechism of the Catholic Church* was still in preparation. This remarkable work is the clear remedy to the situation Piers Paul Read laments. Unfortunately, those who have been in charge of religious education are the ones to whom the dissemination of the Catechism is being entrusted.

This suggests a direction in which the Catholic novelist might go. Once upon a time, Catholic novelists could write against the background of sound doctrine and widespread orthodox practice. No more. The Catholic writer of the future will have the sense of being a guerilla in the service of orthodoxy, with as background a waffling clergy and once-Catholic institutions polemically related to the Vicar of Christ in Rome.

From a purely literary point of view, this is attractive. Catholic novelists used to worry about being thought catechetical, proselytizing under the guise of entertainment. The secular assumption now is that a self-declared Catholic novelist will attack his Church and tell stories about how awful it was to grow up Catholic.

But the assumptions of such novels are disintegrating. The supposed bad old Church is gone. In its place we have strident feminists demanding power, theologians denying the creed, bishops catering to these squeaky wheels, and churches growing emptier by the week.

The emerging situation is one in which such writers as Piers Paul Read can flourish – much to their dismay.

FULTON J. SHEEN

"I should like to know two things – first, what the modern world is thinking about; second, how to answer the errors of modern philosophy in the light of the philosophy of St. Thomas."

In one of my novels there is a school janitor who goes about his duties wearing a headset, listening to Fulton Sheen on tape. How many readers now catch the allusion?

Sheen's tapes are still available, and videos too, that unforgettable voice still at our electronic beck and call. In them he is retreat master, apologist for the faith, expositor of Christian philosophy, a patient, practiced performer whose range and register kept a generation on the edge of their seats. A television star in the first generation of the medium, Fulton Sheen spoke on a set that combined a rectory study and the classroom at The Catholic University where he taught for decades. The books on the studio shelves were props, but the blackboard was functional and often in use.

As a monsignor, he had lectured in a cloak. The first time I saw him was in the auditorium of Holy Angels Academy in Minneapolis. While he was being introduced, he sat in his chair like Lincoln in his monument. When he stood to the welcoming applause, his head was bowed, the dark cloak wrapped tightly about him. And then the arms went out, the crimson lining of the cloak caught the light and seemed to burst into flame, his deep-set eyes swept the audience. "God love you!"

At a certain level of sophistication, it was *de rigueur* not to take Fulton Sheen seriously, to lift a brow at his theatrics, to suggest that he was fine for the groundlings, but . . .

Every teacher simplifies, and Fulton Sheen simplified. But the manner, the histrionics, the studied poses, had a single aim. To convey to his listener the message of Christ. He was a show-off in the service of the Cross.

Like so many other extraordinary churchmen, Fulton Sheen came out of the Peoria diocese. He was born in El Paso – El Paso, Illinois. He was educated at the parish school in Peoria, went on to St. Viator's in Bourbonnais, Illinois (what a salad of languages the Midwest is), completed his preparation for the priesthood at the St. Paul Seminary, and was ordained for Peoria in 1919 at the age of twenty four.

After two years of graduate work at the Catholic University, Sheen became dissatisfied with his progress. A professor asked him what he wanted from his education. "I should like to know two things – first, what the modern world is thinking about; second, how to answer the errors of modern philosophy in the light of the philosophy of St. Thomas." He was advised to go to Louvain in Belgium.

That dual aim captures the point of Leo XIII's *Aeterni Patris*, the encyclical that launched the modern Thomistic revival. The return to Thomas was at once a quest for the truth and for the means to stem the downward slide of modern culture. It was characteristic of Sheen to notice that the name of one of his professors was a palindrome: Leon Noel.

Sheen's unscheduled public debate with S. Alexander, a British philosopher he visited to discuss Alexander's views of God, first put his Thomism to the test. It was Sheen's claim to have read at least once every line Thomas Aquinas wrote.

Sheen retained a youthful look into old age, and it is somewhat surprising to realize he was not an ecclesiastical *wunderkind*. He was nearly forty when he was made a monsignor and fifty-five when he become auxiliary bishop of New York, the elevation following on his being named National Director of the Society for the Propagation of the Faith.

That missionary role followed on Sheen's remarkable history of converts. One of the more famous of them was Clare Booth Luce, author, congresswoman, wife of the founder of the Time-Life empire. The first time they met, when he had asserted the goodness of God, she became angry, shaking a finger under his nose, asking why a good God had permitted her daughter to die. "In order that through that sorrow, you might be here now starting instructions to know Christ and His Church."

Those notables of the time, like Sheen himself, I suppose, have drifted into anonymity. Footnotes would have to identify most of them. A frequent note was the person coming from communism to the faith. From the time of the Spanish Civil War, Fulton Sheen had recognized communism as a spiritual as well as a military menace. *Communism and the Conscience of the West* (1948) is one of the more than sixty books that Sheen published, beginning with *God and Intelligence* in 1925. Along with *Philosophy of Science* (1934) and *Philosophy of Religion* (1948), these are Sheen's most academic books. But from the beginning, he was uninterested in an academic career in the narrow sense. He was a Christian philosopher, a priest, an evangelist. Most of his books convey this pastoral aim.

Sheen took part in Vatican II, and was appointed Bishop of Rochester in 1966 at the age of seventy-two. Three years later, he resigned and was named Titular Archbishop of Newport (Wales). He died in New York City on December 9, 1979. I passed him on the street not long before that. He was coming down Park Avenue toward Grand Central, in the direction of St. Agnes Church, which is located on the street that now bears Sheen's name. I was surprised at how short he seemed. He nodded when I greeted him and there was a flash of the famous smile before he passed on. I had the sense of having seen a celebrity, but it was more than that.

Sheen made a Holy Hour before the Blessed Eucharist every day of his life, keeping a promise he had made on the day he was ordained priest. He tells us too that from the beginning he prayed that he might one day become a bishop. This was not clerical ambition, not in the usual sense. He declined to have his name put forward when the proposal was made early in his life. It was the fullness of the priesthood he wanted, the power to ordain others priest, to be a successor of the apostles.

There has been no one like him since. Perhaps there was no one like him before. He was an original who throughout his life bore the stamp of the Thomist project. To know the truth and to refute error.

Will his books live? A book lives in being read, of course, and I suspect there are not many readers of his output now. Does he deserve readers? Of this there can be little doubt. His books are knowledgeable without being learned. Oh, one comes upon little inaccuracies that annoy – and then is annoyed with himself for exhibiting the pedantry of which Fulton Sheen was incapable.

Perhaps it is only as a performer, as the indefatigable radio speaker and television lecturer, that he lives now. It is not only fictional janitors who are tuned in to that unforgettable voice, speaking to us now from that great studio in the sky. Listen and you will hear his trademark adieu.

God love you!

MURIEL SPARK

"Miss Valvona went to her rest. Many of the grannies followed her. Jean Taylor lingered for a time, employing her pain to magnify the Lord, meditating sometimes confidingly upon Death, the first of the Four Last Things to be ever remembered."

"Long ago in 1945 all the nice people in England were poor, allowing for exceptions." Muriel Spark's *The Girls of Slender Means* is the story of a rooming house in wartime London that might have been an exercise in slick magazine fiction were it not for the author's uncanny knack for suggesting an importance in their doings of which the doers are only imperfectly aware.

I was one of those who was disappointed when Muriel Spark's autobiography *Curriculum Vitae* appeared a couple years ago. On reflection, I realize that my disappointment stemmed from the fact that so much of what she had to tell us about herself she had already used in her fiction. But it was gratifying to be given more on the two enigmatic lines that appear in the little bio in the Penguin edition of her work. "Mrs. Spark became a Roman Catholic in 1954. She has one son."

The son was the fruit of an unwise marriage entered into when she was still in her teens. It took her to Africa where it developed that her husband was insane, and she was lucky to escape with her life. She returned to wartime Britain where her parents looked out for her son, and she went to work in London.

About the conversion she tells us less. Coming out of the Scotland she gives us in *The Prime of Miss Jean Brodie*, Spark would have lived in the atmosphere of religion, and there was a bit of Jewish blood as well. But her conversion seems to have been the catalyst that turned her into a novelist.

All but one or two of her novels are less than the usual length of the genre. *Memento Mori* was her second, and one of its three mottos is taken from the Penny Catechism.

> Q. What are the four last things to be ever remembered?
> A. The four last things to be ever remembered are Death, Judgment, Hell, and Heaven.

The television adaptation of *Memento Mori* brought Muriel Spark to a wide audience who will be glad to hear that there are many more stories every bit as good in Spark's repertoire.

Among those who were dazzled by Spark's debut as a novelist was Evelyn Waugh whose praise is as platinum. Waugh's *The Ordeal of Gilbert Pinfold* appeared at the same time as *Memento Mori* and the older writer was generous – and accurate – enough to say that her book handled their more or less common theme far better than did his. There are important similarities between their work on the level of style and technique.

Mastery in writing is manifest when the writer trusts the scene he puts before us to have the desired effect. The narrator does not react for us, the dialogue is not studded with adverbs or heated substitutes for "he said" and "she said." Like Waugh, Spark can put the grotesque and horrible before us without comment because comment would be superfluous in so artful a narrative.

You might think that this would create the impression of a disengaged narrator, an omniscient onlooker, unmoved by what is being said. But it doesn't. Not only is this the most effective way to achieve an emotional response from the reader – to show what elicits the emotion and trust it will come – it is also a very effective way to suggest the something over and above the surface action which is Muriel Spark's abiding theme. The Four Last Things only make sense if there is a life beyond this one and if what is done here decides what we will be there. Not that Spark is coy about it.

"Miss Valvona went to her rest. Many of the grannies followed her. Jean Taylor lingered for a time, employing her pain to magnify the Lord, meditating sometimes confidingly upon Death, the first of the Four Last Things to be ever remembered."

That is the ending of *Memento Mori*. Here is the end of the *Ballad of Peckham Rye*. A girl married two hours has just said she feels she's been married twenty years.

"He thought this a pity for a girl of eighteen. But it was a sunny day for November, and, as he drove swiftly past the Rye, he saw the children playing there and the women coming home from work with their shopping bags, the Rye for an instant looking like a cloud of green and gold, all the people seeming to ride upon it, as you might say there was another world than this."

Her comic effects are conveyed in the same way, deadpan, trusting the reader to get it.

But emotion and comedy are always lightly at the service of that other world than this one. Like Flannery O'Connor, Muriel Spark is a Catholic writer who does not rely on a lot of Church lore. But it is noteworthy that in a society secularizing itself at a dizzying rate she should insist on making her conversion known.

There was a stretch in her career when Spark got a little too arty for me, employing a sparseness and obliquity that seemed self-referential. What a relief it was when *A Far Cry from Kensington* appeared. We were whisked back into the world of *The Girls of Slender Means*, a world both funnier and sadder and more than itself than that of *The Hot House by the East River*, *The Driver's Seat*, and *Not to Disturb*. Her attempt to transpose Watergate into a convent, *The Abbess of Crewe*, is my least favorite among her novels. It feeds the worldly notion of what the religious life is, and relies for its effect on a very simple version of a complicated partisan frenzy. Still, there is a carryover from that novel to *Symposium*, which it would be difficult not to like. But it was *A Far Cry from Kensington* that reminded me how very good Muriel Spark is.

Is a novelist's imagination tied down to a certain span of years, so that the best work is done when the story is laid then? A case could be made that Waugh's years are the 1930s but I would not agree: it is the period of World War II. I think the same is true of Spark; it is the London of wartime, life lived under the constant threat of falling bombs, mortal danger as ordinary as getting up and going to work.

"So great was the noise during the day that I used to lie awake at night listening to the silence. Eventually, I fell asleep contented, filled with soundlessness, but while I was awake I enjoyed the experience of darkness, thought, memory, sweet anticipations. I heard the silence."

That is the sound of a writer returning to the country of her imagination, and it prepares us for the quirky, funny, frightening things to follow, a deft and lightly told story that puts us in mind of so much more. The Four Last Things, for example.

EDITH STEIN

But the universal appeal of this saintly woman lies in her abiding and personal pursuit of the truth. "This is the truth," she said when she put down the autobiography of Teresa. The next step was obvious. She must become a Catholic.

In a letter written during World War I, Edith Stein could say "that there has never been as strong a consciousness of being a state as there is in Prussia and the new German Reich. That is why I consider it out of the question that we will now be defeated." During the same period (already a Doctor of Philosophy, she was research assistant to Edmund Husserl) she wrote that "to be at the service of a person, in short – to obey, is something I cannot do." Twenty-four years later, in 1942, A Carmelite nun, vowed to poverty, chastity, and obedience, she was executed at Auschwitz under the anti-Jewish laws of the expiring Third Reich.

Edith Stein was canonized in 1998 by Pope John Paul II under the name she took when she entered the Carmelites, Sister Teresa Benedicta a Cruce. She is a powerful symbol of the mystery of the Jewish people. Her memoir, *Life in a Jewish Family 1891–1916*, like her recollection of her first studies at the University of GÖttingen, puts before her reader Jews who are completely assimilated, Germans among Germans. Edith lost her religious faith as a university student but continued to attend synagogue with her devout widowed mother. She became absorbed in philosophy, the phenomenology of Husserl, until, as the result of reading the autobiography of St. Teresa of Avila, she entered the Catholic Church to the great sorrow of her mother. She was baptized on January 1, 1922, not yet thirty-one years old.

There seemed little doubt that Edith Stein would eventually be canonized, and so she was. It is imaginable that she will be declared a Doctor of the Church (which would give us a triad of Carmelite Theresas so designated). Many of her writings are of interest only to philosophers, but her role in the Church is surely not confined to them.

It was not until 1933 that Edith stopped teaching, because of the Nazi laws against Jews, and entered the Carmelite convent in Cologne. This brilliant, gifted woman, who had been engaged in scholarly study and writing, had no reason to think that this would continue in the convent. Thomas Merton gave up his worldly ambition to become a writer when he became a Trappist and the laurel that had eluded him as a layman came to him as a monk. But Edith Stein had already made her mark as a scholar prior to becoming a nun. It is one of the great blessings of her life – I mean blessing for us – that she was urged to continue her philosophical writing.

The masterpiece she wrote, *Finite and Eternal Being*, could not be published at the time because of her Jewish origins, but eventually it was. It is a work of breathtaking scope, comparable to St. Thomas Aquinas's *Summa Contra Gentes*. In a comprehensive *tour de monde* embracing the natural and supernatural, Edith Stein exhibits her training as a phenomenologist as well as her immersion in the thought of Aquinas after her conversion.

She wrote as well *The Science of the Cross*, a study on St. John of the Cross, and various other spiritual works which are gradually finding their way into print. *Essays on Woman* contains talks and articles written during the decade prior to her entrance into Carmel.

Edith Stein is a model for the Catholic philosopher. Once she had entered the Church, although she was a fully formed thinker, she became as a little student again when she began to study

St. Thomas Aquinas. Those who overlook and even disdain the Church's reiterated recommendation of Thomas Aquinas as our mentor in theology and philosophy are rebuked by the docility of this brilliant woman. That the study of Thomas was philosophically and theologically fruitful is everywhere evident in her Catholic writings.

But the universal appeal of this saintly woman lies in her abiding and personal pursuit of the truth. "This is the truth," she said when she put down the autobiography of Teresa. The next step was obvious. She must become a Catholic. She studied the catechism and missal and presented herself at the rectory door, to the astonishment of the priest who quizzed her on her knowledge of the faith.

Saintly people are singled out by the Church because they have something special to tell us about what it means to be a Christian. It could be argued that the great significance of Edith Stein for the present lies in her wise reflection on what it means to be a Christian woman in the modern world.

Others would argue that her exemplary role is to be found in her intellectual labors, her philosophical and theological contribution.

Some would seek her significance in something more universal, in the quest for sanctity at a stage of history that seems to have lost all sense of God.

Phenomenology is a mode of philosophy that brought many to the faith. Behind its forbidding façade, it retains the original conception of philosophy as the pursuit of wisdom, as a way of life. *Primum vivere, deinde philosophari* (live first, then philosophize) is a maxim that has its importance. But more important still is the realization that to philosophize truly is to live more truly.

It was the hunger and thirst for truth that brought Edith Stein to Christ and to the Cross. She offered her death at Auschwitz for the Jewish people. Recently, there was controversy over the location of a Carmelite Convent there where Edith Stein and so many others had been so brutally slain, some Jews taking offense at the cross that had been raised on the site.

Edith Stein would have understood. The Cross is always a sign of contradiction. It is also our only hope.

EVELYN WAUGH

In Brideshead Revisited, written during a war-time leave, Waugh set out to write the obituary of the doomed English upper class. It was only after he had finished his magnificent World War II trilogy Sword of Honour in 1961 that he realized he had written another obituary, that of the Roman Catholic Church in England as it had existed for centuries.

At the end of his novella *Scott-King's Modern Europe*, Evelyn Waugh's hero remarks, "I think it would be very wicked indeed to do anything to fit a boy for the modern world." This was in 1946 when Waugh's career as a novelist was not quite two decades old and when he had exactly twenty years more of life.

Once it was fashionable to dismiss Waugh as a curmudgeon who dearly loved a lord and could not or would not adjust to the realities of socialist Britain. He did say he found it possible to go on living in his native land only by imagining he was a tourist. In this negative attitude toward the way we live now, Waugh seems merely to have beat the rush, but as always with this deep and subtle man there is so much more than conservative grumbling about confiscatory taxation to finance the welfare state. Waugh was a tourist here in the way every Catholic is – he was *in via*.

His early novels are disarming. In a style midway between that of Ronald Firbank and P. G. Wodehouse, Waugh wrote of bright young things, heedless, mindless aesthetes who careened about London in what seemed a prelapsarian fashion. The early novels are autobiographical, the author relates to them somewhat as F. Scott Fitzgerald related to his first two novels and innumerable short stories in which the Jazz Age is featured. The Jazz Age, like

Waugh's Metroland, turns out to be a world of despair, where winter dreams die and we can be shown fear in a handful of dust.

An argument could be made that *Handful of Dust* is Waugh's greatest novel. For the first time, it became unmistakable that he was an extremely serious writer who needed the comic to make his vision of life bearable. Tony Last – the last of a line, one who sticks to his last, a survivor into a strange time – is the one moral man in a world of insouciant betrayals. In the end, all the other characters end up well, but Tony is last seen in a Latin American jungle, the prisoner of an illiterate madman to whom he must read the works of Dickens over and over and over. The juxtaposition of the sentimentalized Christianity of Dickens and the jungle clearing is eloquent.

In *Brideshead Revisited*, written during a war-time leave, Waugh set out to write the obituary of the doomed English upper class. It was only after he had finished his magnificent World War II trilogy *Sword of Honour* in 1961 that he realized he had written another obituary, that of the Roman Catholic Church in England as it had existed for centuries. It had never occurred to him, he said, that the Church was susceptible to change. "I was wrong and I have seen a superficial revolution in what then seemed permanent."

Waugh was a convert who took his new faith with the utmost seriousness. It is altogether typical of him that, in the preface to *Helena*, he countered the quip that if all the pieces of the true Cross were put together the result would be an enormity, by citing the calculations of Charles Rohault de Fleury to show we have a mere fraction of the Cross's presumed size. "As far as volume goes, therefore, there is no strain on the credulity of the faithful." He wrote lives of Edmund Campion the martyr and of Ronald Knox. Like most Englishman, he had a snooty attitude toward the United States, manifest in *The Loved One*, for example, but there was one great exception.

In 1946, in a long article for *Life*, Waugh predicted an American epoch in the Catholic Church. Like Jacques Maritain, he was impressed by the phenomenal rise in contemplative vocations after the war; Waugh himself edited the English version of Thomas Merton's autobiography. At about this same time, he predicted that Monsignor Knox's translation of the Bible would be the standard version for ages to come. Prophesy was not among Waugh's gifts. Vatican II came as a great shock to him, not so much the Council as its implementation.

"I am now old but I was young when I was received into the Church. . . . One of the extraneous attractions of the Church which most drew me was the spectacle of the priest and his server at low Mass, stumping up to the altar without a glance to discover how many or how few he had in his congregation; a craftsman and his apprentice; a man with a job which he alone was qualified to do. That is the Mass I have grown to know and love. By all means let the rowdy have their 'dialogues,' but let us who value silence not be completely forgotten."

When Donat Gallagher collected the essays, articles, and reviews of Evelyn Waugh, he appended a list of the writings he did not include. There are a dozen articles which appeared in the *Tablet*, the *Catholic Herald*, and *Commonweal* during and immediately after Vatican II which if collected would be an important contribution to the history of the post-conciliar Church.

Waugh was a writer of consummate skill. He came to deplore the fruity excesses he had permitted himself in *Brideshead*. In everything else, his mature style is a model of clarity, simplicity and brilliance. We have his novels, his travel books, his biographies, his journalism, his diaries, and his letters. He was a very productive writer who earned his living with his pen. Like the priest, he had a job to do, and no other Catholic writer of the 20th century did it any better than Evelyn Waugh. He died at the age of sixty three on Easter Sunday, 1966. Finally Waugh and peace had met.

HANDFULS OF DUST

Yet another life of Evelyn Waugh has appeared, this one by Selina Hastings, a friend of the author who puts before herself the twofold task of giving her reader an impression of what it was like to know Waugh and what it was like to be Waugh. Piers Paul Read, in reviewing the book in the *London Times* (October 27, 1994), says she has accomplished the first but only God could do the second.

The very fact that this is the third major biography (and more were to follow) of the curmudgeonly Catholic convert suggests how elusive the life of another can be, even the life of a somewhat public figure. Waugh left a huge diary, which has been published, and many letters of which several collections have appeared. By all accounts Waugh could be rude, he suffered fools not at all, and he was given to self-indulgence in matters of food and drink. But what strikes me in reading his letters is his generosity – he seemed forever to be giving someone money or help of one kind of another, unobtrusively. And he was merciless with himself. Biographers can tell us unfavorable stories about him because he told them first.

Waugh, when asked by someone how he could act the way he did and claim to be a Catholic, replied that his critic might consider how much worse he would be if he weren't a Catholic.

Because Waugh himself is the source of much of what we know about him, we must be careful in interpreting the information. Writers are notoriously unreliable as witnesses of autobiographical fact. It is not that they lie, but something of imaginative shaping enters into their accounts of themselves.

It doesn't matter. The essential life of others is closed to us. Indeed, we are mysteries to ourselves. Sir James Barrie said that life is a book in which we set out to write one story and end by writing another. Novels are books deliberately written in quest of the wonder of the human person whose life is inevitably a mixture of the intended and unintended but with the suggestion of a pattern of whose meaning we are never quite sure. For most of us, it is this realization that makes us aware of the hand of God in our lives. The poet, the novelist, the saint above all, remind us how little our fate is in our hands.

If nothing else, turbulence at thirty thousand feet can bring it forcibly home. Or reading a little Waugh.